A Book of
Lenten Prayers

A Book of
Lenten Prayers

✝

Composed, edited, and translated by
William G. Storey
Professor Emeritus of Liturgy
University of Notre Dame

LOYOLA PRESS.
A JESUIT MINISTRY
Chicago

LOYOLAPRESS.
A JESUIT MINISTRY

3441 N. Ashland Avenue
Chicago, Illinois 60657
(800) 621-1008
www.loyolapress.com

Copyright acknowledgments appear on pages 169–171 and constitute a continuation of this copyright page.

Photo credits:
p. v Shroud of Turin Wikipedia: US-PD
p. 83 Shroud of Turin (detail) Wikipedia: US-PD

Library of Congress Cataloging-in-Publication Data
Storey, William George, 1923-
  A book of Lenten prayers / composed, edited, and translated by William G. Storey.
    p. cm.
  Includes bibliographical references
  ISBN-13: 978-0-8294-3825-3
  ISBN-10: 0-8294-3825-4
1. Lent--Prayers and devotions. I. Title.
  BV85.S73 2013
  242'.802--dc23

                                                    2012029441

Printed in the United States of America.
12 13 14 15 16 17 18 Bang 10 9 8 7 6 5 4 3 2 1

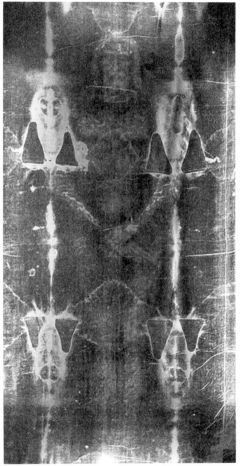

Shroud of Turin

To David Boudreau, O.F.M. Cap.
of the Capuchins of Eastern Canada

Contents

4. Resurrection and Ascension 97

The Five Hours of the Resurrection:
A Little Office of the Risen Christ 108

A Devotion to the Risen Christ 145

1
Praying the Easter Mysteries: Jesus' Dying and Rising

The Paschal Mystery

"The world turns
but the Cross stands unmoved."[1]

The Christian Passover is as important to us as the Jewish Passover was and is to the Jews. By God's saving power Israel was liberated from the slavery of Egypt, guided through the Desert of Sinai, and brought into the Promised Land as the chosen people of God. The new people of God in the New Testament are set free from sin and death by the paschal mystery of Jesus' dying and rising, and made the new people of God.

Centuries before the church developed Holy Week and the Sacred Triduum, churches celebrated the paschal mystery every week. Christians celebrated the glorious resurrection of Jesus on the Lord's Day (Sunday) and his passion and death on Friday. Sometimes Sunday is called a "little Easter," but the better term would be "the original Easter." The Lord's Supper on the Lord's Day is the first day of the week and, despite its attrition by the secular world, the Sunday Eucharist is still the center of the week for all believing Christians.

This is one great mystery of our redemption spread over three days each week—Friday, Saturday, Sunday—without separation or division, the cross bleeding into the resurrection, conducting us from death to life, from earth to heaven.

The Turning Point

The Cross is the dramatic about face from the old to the new. This means not only turning away from the Old Testament but a turning away from the whole of the decaying of the old world; and it is not only a turning to the Church (which will be the visible sacrament of reconciliation with God), but to the whole of the new world which is here being born and which is to be perfected at creation's final transfiguration. The Cross is the turning point, the transition, the Passover. And in the turning point—the Crucified—both things coincide: God's fury, which will make no compromises with sin but can only reject it and turn it into ashes, and God's love, which it begins to reveal itself precisely at the place of this inexorable confrontation.

Hans Urs von Balthasar (1905–1988)[2]

The cosmic renewal that ensued makes the cross the very center of the Catholic religion, its liturgy, and its most important forms of piety. Jesus calls upon us to believe in the mystery of faith, to celebrate it in the Holy Eucharist, and to *heighten* both faith and liturgy by the traditional forms of Christian devotion that reinforce our spiritual understanding of the paschal mystery and its continuing impact on our lives each day.

Let us recall the words of St. Gertrude of Helfta (1256–ca. 1302), a major mystic of the late thirteenth century, who received this instruction from the Lord when she was thinking about the Lord's passion:

> *She understood that meditations on the prayers or passages of Scripture which deal with the Lord's passion are infinitely more efficacious than any others. As it is impossible to touch flour without getting dusty, so no one can think about the Lord's passion with any devotion and not derive some fruit from it. Indeed, even if one only reads something about the passion, one is preparing one's soul to receive at least some of its fruits; for the intention of a person who calls to mind the passion of Christ bears more fruit than the many intentions of another who pays no heed to the Lord's passion. Let us try, therefore, to turn over in our minds more frequently the subject of Christ's passion, so that it may be for us "honey in the mouth, music in the ear, gladness in the heart."*[3]

Our Habits of Prayer

Let us attend to another major mystic, Blessed Julian of Norwich (ca. 1342–ca. 1416), on the intermediaries that God provides us to pray out of his goodness:

There came to mind then how numerous were all these different ways of prayer: how we are wont to pray to God by his holy Flesh, by his precious Blood, or his holy Passion—his most dear Death, his honorable Wounds. But the blessings, and eternal life that stems from this, all come from the same goodness of God. It is the same when we pray to him for love of his sweet Mother who bore him: this too is from God's goodness. Or we might pray by the holy Cross on which he died; but all the power and help that derives from that cross, this again is of his goodness. And so it is also with all the special help we have from the saints and all the company of heaven, that is to say the very dear love and the never ending friendship we have with them: it is of his goodness. The means afforded by the goodness of God are so plentiful in number; but chief among them is the blessed kind that he took to himself of the Maiden, together with all the means that belong to our redemption and our endless salvation both before and after.[4]

In most of the devotions in this book, the readings are central to our meditations. The most important readings are from holy scripture and then, secondarily, from the Fathers and Mothers of the Church and other Christian authors. Not all of these are meant to be read each time—make your own choices—but all of them contain nuggets of insight and wisdom. The hymns, psalms, canticles, litanies, and prayers are supporting partners to the passages of scripture. The more we grasp their meaning the more we are in partnership with them.

2
The Season of Lent

From Ash Wednesday through the Thursday Morning of Holy Week

The forty days of Lent were originally established in the fourth century to prepare those who were to be baptized during the Easter Vigil. This season still carries that emphasis, both for those about to be initiated and for those who are going to renew their baptismal vows at Easter.

Inspired by the example and fervor of such new Christians, the baptized want to renew their commitment to Christ too and to promise again to live up to their baptismal promises. New Christians and old Christians meet together in faith during Lent and, above all, during the Easter Vigil. The former are immersed in water and the Holy Spirit and made new creatures in Christ, while the latter renew and reaffirm their baptism through repentance and the public renewal of their baptismal vows. The climax is the celebration of the Easter Eucharist and the union of all at the altar in Holy Communion.

Traditionally, Lent calls for three observances: prayer, fasting, and almsgiving—*prayer* to fix the mind on Christ and the Gospel message; *fasting* to help the body share in the sufferings of Jesus and of the poor; and *almsgiving* to set aside money for those in need. Almsgiving includes gifts of time and money and commitment to the corporal and spiritual works of mercy.

The *corporal works of mercy* are feed the hungry, give drink to the thirsty, clothe the naked, shelter the homeless, visit the sick, visit prisoners, bury the dead.

The *spiritual works of mercy* are counsel the doubtful, instruct the ignorant, admonish sinners, comfort the afflicted, forgive offenses, bear wrongs patiently, pray for the living and the dead.

This devotional prayer book emphasizes the graces of Baptism and Penance, as Vatican II teaches:

> *The two elements which are especially characteristic of Lent—the recalling of Baptism or the preparation for it, and Penance—should be given greater emphasis in the liturgy and in liturgical catechesis. It is by them that the Church prepares attentively to God's word and more time to prayer.*[5]

In addition this book centers on the traditional devotions that concentrate on the great passing over from the cross to the unique new life of the Risen Christ. It contains devotions to the Holy Face of Jesus, Friday and Sunday devotions to the paschal mystery, the Five Hours of the Holy Cross, the Five Hours of the Resurrection, a Devotion to the Paschal Mystery, a Devotion to the Risen Christ, a devotion to the Sorrowful Mother, and other devotions to the Resurrection and the Ascension.

Ash Wednesday opens this season. Many parishioners also attend daily Mass during Lent, observe the now minimal fast days of Ash Wednesday, Good Friday, and perhaps Holy Saturday, make the Way of the Cross in private or in common on Fridays, and still observe some of the devotions found in this book.

The Church repeats these words today [on Ash Wednesday] as she traces the ashen cross upon our foreheads: "Remember you are dust, and into dust you will return." Thus the Church strikes the opening chord of a symphony that will resound through all the weeks of Lent, until, in the Easter Vigil, it swells to its thrilling climax: "Happy that fault that won so great and glorious a Redeemer." Humbly, then, yet full of confidence, we go to the altar today to receive the ashes upon our foreheads. We are humble because we realize our sinful condition, we who must daily fight against the flesh, surrounded all our lives by sorrow, sin, temptation and evil. But we are full of confidence, grace, and in the sign of the Cross and the triumphant power of grace we shall achieve the victory."

Pius Parsch (1884–1954)

If a parish is to have baptisms of catechumens during the Easter Vigil, there will be several special observances on certain Lenten Sundays. The catechumens who participate in these ceremonies need their fellow parishioners to support them in faith and participate in these common events. All members of the congregation are invited to support them by friendship, prayer, and fasting. Usually the parish also offers Penance services for the baptized. This Rite of Reconciliation is especially helpful before Easter for those who have fallen away from the Church and/or are involved in mortal sin. But it is also good for average parishioners who need greater sensitivity to sin and failure.

Lenten observances are needed for all of us and the following devotions will assist us in doing so.

The Seven Penitential Psalms

Almost a thousand years ago, these seven psalms were selected by our Catholic ancestors to help them to wipe away both venial and even more serious sins. When the Books of Hours appeared in the twelfth century, the seven psalms became one of their normal features and were often given to penitents in confession as their assigned penance.

The seven psalms are prayed kneeling before a crucifix by a group or by a single person. "He [a penitent] must fall prostrate before God, keeping in front of him 'some pitiful image of Christ's bitter passion,' and there confess all his faults."[6]

They are helpful for all of us and may be used in several ways: the group of seven may be used each day of the week: as one psalm each day of a week; as three sets of psalms with the three prayers in honor of the Holy Cross; or as a special preparation before confession or as a penance after it.

The three prayers attached to the seven penitential psalms are taken from The Monastic Agreement of the Monks and Nuns of the English Nation issued during the reign of King Edgar (959–975).[7]

The leader of prayer begins the Antiphon to the asterisk and all continue it.

ANTIPHON O Lord, remember me * AND LOOK FAVORABLY UPON ME. DO NOT PUNISH ME FOR MY SINS.

Psalm 6 Domine, ne in furore tuo arguas me

O Lord, do not rebuke me in your anger,
 nor chasten me in your wrath.
Be gracious to me, O Lord, for I languish;
 O Lord, heal me, for my bones are stricken.
My whole being also is stricken with terror.
But you, O Lord—how long?

Turn, O Lord, save my life;
 deliver me for the sake of your steadfast love.
For in death there is no remembrance of you;
 in Sheol who can give you praise?

I am weary with my moaning;
 every night I flood my bed with tears;
 I drench my couch with my weeping.
My eyes waste away because of grief,
 they grow weak with all my foes.

Depart from me, all you workers of evil,
  for the Lord has heard the sound
    of my weeping.
The Lord has heard my supplication;
  the Lord accepts my prayer.

All my enemies shall be ashamed
    and stricken with terror;
  they shall turn back, and be put
    to shame in a moment.

Glory to the Father, and to the Son,
  and to the Holy Spirit:
as it was in the beginning, is now,
  and will be for ever. Amen.

Psalm 32 *Beati, quorum remissae sunt*

Blessed are those whose transgression is forgiven,
  whose sin is covered.
Blessed are those whom the Lord does not hold
        guilty,
  and in whose spirit there is no deceit.

When I did not declare my sin, my body wasted
        away
  through my groaning all day long.
For day and night your hand was heavy upon me;
  my strength was dried up as by the heat of
        summer.

I acknowledged my sin to you,
  and I did not hide my iniquity;

I said, "I will confess my transgressions to the
    Lord;"
  then you forgave the guilt of my sin.

Therefore those who are godly
  offer prayer to you;
at a time of distress, the rush of great waters
  shall not reach them.

You are a hiding place for me,
  you preserve me from trouble;
  you encompass me with deliverance.
I will instruct you and teach you
  the way you should go;
  I will counsel you with my eye upon you.

Do not be like an unruly horse or a mule,
    without understanding,
  whose temper must be curbed
    with bit and bridle.

Many are the pangs of the wicked;
  but steadfast love surrounds those
    who trust in the Lord.
Be glad in the Lord, and rejoice, O righteous;
  shout for joy, all you upright in heart!

Glory to the Father, and to the Son,
  and to the Holy Spirit:
as it was in the beginning, is now,
  and will be for ever. Amen.

Psalm 38 Domine, ne in furore tuo

O Lord, do not rebuke me in your anger,
  nor punish me in your wrath!
For your arrows have sunk in me,
  and your hand has come down on me.

There is no soundness in my flesh
  because of your indignation;
there is no health in my bones
  because of my sin.

For my iniquities have invaded my head;
  they weigh like a burden too heavy for me.
My wounds grow foul and fester
  because of my foolishness,
I am utterly bowed down and prostrate;
  all day I go about mourning.

For my loins are filled with burning,
  and there is no soundness in my flesh.
I am utterly spent and crushed;
  I groan because of the tumult of my heart.

Lord, all my longing is known to you,
  my sighing is not hidden from you.
My heart throbs, my strength fails me;
  even the light of my eyes has gone out.

My friends and companions stand aloof
    from my sickness,
  and my neighbors stand far off.

Those who seek my life lay their snares,
  those who seek to hurt me speak of ruin,
  and plot treachery all day long.

But I am like the deaf, I do not hear,
  like the mute who does not speak.
Truly, I am like one who does not hear,
  and in whose mouth is no retort.

But I wait for you, O Lord;
  you will answer, O Lord, my God!
For I pray, "Let them not rejoice over me,
  who boast against me when my foot slips!"

For I am ready to fall,
  and my pain is ever with me.
I confess my iniquity,
  I am sorry for my sin.

Those who are my foes without cause are mighty,
  and many of those who hate me wrongfully.
Those who render me evil for good
  oppose me because I follow after good.

Do not forsake me, O Lord!
  O my God, be not far from me!
Make haste to help me,
  O Lord, my salvation.

Glory to the Father, and to the Son,
  and to the Holy Spirit:
as it was in the beginning, is now,
  and will be for ever. Amen.

First Prayer in Honor of the Holy Cross

Lord Jesus Christ,
  I worship you mounting the Cross;
  I implore you that the cross may free me
  from the deceits of the devil.
Lord Jesus Christ, I worship you wounded
    on the Cross;
  I implore you that your wounds
  may be the healing of my soul.
Lord Jesus Christ, I worship you laid
    in the grave;
  I implore you that your death be my life.
Lord Jesus Christ,
  I worship you descending into hell
  to set free those in prison there;
  I implore you not to let me to come there.
Lord Jesus Christ,
I worship you rising from the grave
  and ascending into heaven;
  I implore you to have mercy on me.
Lord Jesus Christ,
  I worship you when you come in judgment;
  I implore you, at your coming not to judge me,
  but to forgive rather than to condemn.
You live and reign with the Father,
in the unity of the Holy Spirit,
one God, for ever and ever.
~Amen.

Psalm 51:1–17 Miserere mei, Deus

Have mercy on me, O God,
  according to your steadfast love;
according to your abundant mercy
  blot out my transgressions.
Wash me thoroughly from my iniquity,
  and cleanse me from my sin!

For I know my transgressions,
  and my sin is ever before me.
Against you, you only, I have sinned,
  and done that which is evil in your sight,
so that you are justified in your sentence
  and blameless in your judgment.

Surely, you desire truth in the inward being;
  therefore you teach me wisdom in my secret
      heart.
Purge me with hyssop, and I shall be clean;
  wash me, and I shall be whiter than snow;

Let me hear with joy and gladness;
  let the bones which you have broken rejoice.
Hide your face from my sins,
  and blot out all my iniquities.

Create in me a clean heart, O God,
  and put a new and right spirit within me.
Cast me not away from your presence,
  and take not your holy spirit from me.

Restore to me the joy of your salvation,
  and sustain in me a willing spirit.
Then I will teach transgressors your ways,
  and sinners will return to you.

Deliver me from bloodshed, O God,
    God of my salvation,
  and my tongue will sing aloud
    of your deliverance.

O Lord, open my lips,
  and my mouth shall show forth your praise.
For you have no delight in sacrifice;
  were I to give a burnt offering, you would
    not be pleased.
The sacrifice acceptable to God is a broken spirit;
  A broken and contrite heart, O God,
    you will not despise.

Glory to the Father, and to the Son,
  and to the Holy Spirit:
as it was in the beginning, is now,
  and will be for ever. Amen.

Psalm 102 *Domine, exaudi orationem meam*

Hear my prayer, O Lord;
  let my cry come to you!
Do not hide your face from me
  in the day of my distress!

Listen to me;
  answer me speedily in the day when I call!

For my days pass away like smoke,
  and my bones burn like a furnace.

My heart is withered like dried up grass;
  I am too wasted to eat my bread.
Because of my loud groaning
  my bones cling to my flesh.

I am like an owl in the wilderness,
  like a little owl of the waste places.
I lie awake,
  I am like a lonely bird on a housetop.

All day long my enemies taunt me,
  those who deride me use my name for a curse.
For I eat ashes like bread,
  and mingle my tears with my drink,
because of your indignation and anger;
  for you have lifted me up and thrown me away.
My days are like an evening shadow;
  I wither like grass.

But you, O Lord, are enthroned forever;
  your name endures to all generations.
You will arise and have pity on Zion;
  it is time to favor it;
  the appointed time has come.

For your servants hold its stones dear,
  and have pity on its dust.
The nations will fear the name of the Lord,
  and all the kings of the earth your glory.

For the Lord will build up Zion,
  and gloriously will appear;
the Lord will turn toward the prayer
    of the destitute
  and will not despise their prayer.

Let this be recorded for a generation to come,
  so that a people yet unborn may praise the Lord:
that the Lord looked down from a holy height,
  from heaven the Lord looked at the earth,
to hear the groans of the prisoners
  to set free those who were doomed to die;
that the name of the Lord may be declared in
      Zion,
  and God's praise in Jerusalem,
when peoples and kingdoms gather together
    to worship the Lord.

The Lord has broken my strength in mid-course,
  and has shortened my days.
"O my God," I say, "do not take me away
  in the midst of my days,
  you whose years endure
  throughout all the generations!"

Long ago you laid the foundations of the earth,
  and the heavens are the work of your hands.
They will perish, but you endure;
  they will all wear out like a garment.

You change them like clothing, and they pass
　　away;
　but you are the same, and your years have no
　　end.
The children of your servants shall dwell secure;
　their posterity shall be established before you.

Glory to the Father, and to the Son,
　and to the Holy Spirit:
as it was in the beginning, is now,
　and will be for ever. Amen.

THE SECOND PRAYER IN HONOR OF THE HOLY CROSS

Lord Jesus Christ,
glorious Creator of the world,
splendor of the Father's glory,
co-eternal with Him and the Holy Spirit;
Who deigned to take flesh of the spotless Virgin
and permitted your glorious hands to be fixed
to the gibbet of the Cross
that you might overthrow the gates of hell
and free the human race from everlasting death;
look down and have mercy on me,
a wretch borne down by the weight of sin from
　　heaven
and polluted by the stains of my many misdeeds:
in your mercy do not forsake me, most loving
　　Father,

but forgive that which I have sinned most
    disloyally.
Hear me prostrate before your adorable
and most glorious Cross that I may stand before
    you
pure and pleasing in your sight,
who reigns with the Father,
in the unity of the Holy Spirit,
one God, for ever and ever.
~Amen.

Psalm 130 *De profundis clamavi ad te*

Out of the depths I cry to you, O Lord!
  Lord, hear my voice!
Let your ears be attentive
  to the voice of my supplications!

If you, O Lord, should mark iniquities,
  Lord, who could stand.
But there is forgiveness with you,
  that you may be worshipped.

I wait for the Lord, my soul waits,
  in the Lord's word I hope;
my soul waits for the Lord
  more than watchers for the morning,
  more than watchers for the morning.

O Israel, hope in the Lord!
  For with the Lord there is steadfast love;

with the Lord there is great redemption.
The Lord alone will redeem Israel
  from all iniquities.

Glory to the Father, and to the Son,
  and to the Holy Spirit:
as it was in the beginning, is now,
  and will be for ever. Amen.

Psalm 143 *Domine, exaudi orationem meam*

Hear my prayer, O Lord;
  in your faithfulness listen to my supplications;
  in your righteousness answer me!
Do not enter into judgment with your servant;
  for no one living is righteous before you.

For enemies have pursued me;
  they have crushed my life to the ground;
  they have made me sit in darkness like those
      long dead.
Therefore my spirit faints within me;
  my heart within me is appalled.

I remember the days of old,
  I meditate on all your deeds;
  I muse on the works of your hands.
I stretch out my hands to you;
  my life thirsts for you like a parched land.

Make haste to answer me, O Lord!
  My spirit fails!

Do not hide your face from me,
　or I shall be like those who go down to the pit.

In the morning let me hear of your steadfast love,
　for in you I put my trust.
Teach me the way I should go,
　for to you I lift up my life.

Save me, O Lord, from my enemies!
　I have fled to you for refuge!
Teach me to do your will,
　for you are my God!

Let your good Spirit lead me
　on a level path!
For your name's sake, O Lord, preserve my life.
　In your righteousness bring me out of trouble.
In your steadfast love cut off my enemies,
　and destroy all my adversaries,
　for I am your servant.

Glory to the Father, and to the Son,
　and to the Holy Spirit:
as it was in the beginning, is now,
　and will be for ever. Amen.

ANTIPHON O LORD, REMEMBER ME AND LOOK
　FAVORABLY UPON ME. DO NOT PUNISH ME FOR
　MY SINS.

THIRD PRAYER IN HONOR OF THE HOLY CROSS

Almighty God, Lord Jesus Christ,
who for our sake stretched out
your pure hands on the cross
and redeemed us with your precious Blood,
grant me to feel and understand
    that I have true repentance
and great perseverance all the days of my life.
Your reign is a reign for all ages.
~AMEN.

3
The Paschal Mystery

Just as Moses lifted up the serpent in the wilderness, so must the Son of Man be lifted up, that whoever believes in him may have eternal life.

John 3:14–15

Look! He is coming with the clouds; every eye will see him, even those who pierced him; and on his account all the tribes of the earth will wail. "I am the Alpha and Omega," says the Lord God, "who is and who was and who is to come, the Almighty. When they look on the one whom they have pierced, they shall all mourn for him, as one mourns for an only child."

Revelation 1:7–8; John 19:37; Zechariah 12:10–11

Wherever we visit a Catholic church and many Catholic homes, we find ourselves facing a crucifix. It is usually the dying or dead figure of Christ nailed to the cross, but sometimes it is the risen and glorified Christ standing on or in front of the cross. Whichever form it takes, the crucifix is the central image/symbol/sign of Catholic Christianity.

Most Christian scholars agree that the last few chapters of each Gospel were the first to be composed—that is, the ones containing the most obvious mysteries of Jesus' life, his passion, death, and resurrection. Indeed, the four Gospels may be considered as accounts of the Passion of Jesus preceded by fairly lengthy introductions. The central fact is that the paschal mystery is the very essence and center of our redemptive history—and of our devotional life.

Listen to the Lord Jesus:

THE YOKE OF JESUS　　　　　MATTHEW 11:28–30

"Come to me, all you that are weary and are carrying heavy burdens, and I will give you rest. Take my yoke upon you, and learn from me; for I am gentle and humble in heart, and you will find rest for your souls. For my yoke is easy, and my burden is light."

TAKE UP YOUR CROSS　　　　　MATTHEW 16:24–26

Jesus told his disciples, "If any want to become my followers, let them deny themselves and take up their cross and follow me. For those who want to save their life will lose it, and those who lose their life for my sake will find it. For what will it profit them if they gain the whole world but forfeit their life? Or what will they give in return for their life?"

Just as Moses lifted up the serpent in the wilderness, so must the Son of Man be lifted up, that whoever believes in him may have eternal life. For God so loved the world that he gave his only Son, so that everyone who believes in him may not perish but may have eternal life. The Father loves the Son and has placed all things in his hand. Whoever believes in the Son has eternal life; whoever disobeys the Son will not see life, but must endure God's wrath.

THE HOLY CROSS

Christ when he died
Deceived the cross;
And on death's side
Threw all the loss.
The captive world awaked and found
The prisoner loose, the jailer bound.

Richard Crashaw (ca. 1613–1649)[8]

The Veneration of the Cross at Jerusalem

According to a reliable tradition, St. Helena, the mother of Constantine the Great, on pilgrimage to Jerusalem (ca. 325), discovered the cross that Jesus died on, the nails, the title, and the empty tomb in which his body reposed for three days. The emperor built one of the most magnificent churches in the world to house these sacred treasures where pilgrims venerated the holy cross and the empty tomb.

Here is a fourth-century description by the pilgrim Egeria who spent three years in Jerusalem (382–386) and saw the bishop of Jerusalem present the holy cross to the hundreds and later thousands for their veneration on Good Friday morning.

> *[After an all-night vigil the bishop urges the people to sit for a while and then reassemble]" at eight o'clock so that till midday you can see the holy Wood of the Cross, which, as every one of us believes, helps us attain salvation.*
>
> *The bishop's chair is placed on Golgotha Behind the Cross, where he now stands, and he takes his seat. A table is placed before him with a cloth on it, the deacons stand round, and there is brought to him a gold and silver box containing the holy Wood of the Cross. It is opened and the Wood of the Cross and the Title are taken out and placed on the table.*
>
> *Thus all the people go past one by one. They stoop down, touch the holy Wood first with their forehead and then with their eyes, and then kiss it, but no one puts out his hand to touch it . . . and till noon everybody goes by, entering by one door and going out through the other, till midday.*[9]

This fourth-century veneration of the true cross soon swept the Catholic world even where there were no pieces of the holy wood. The Good Friday Roman liturgy of the twenty-first century is a direct descendant of this custom as millions venerate a replica of the true cross in their parish churches.

Brief Devotions to Christ Crucified

These devotions are offered for Lent and more especially for Holy Week. They are also useful throughout the year and especially for Fridays.

Faith and Trust in Jesus Crucified

This great prayer of the preeminent martyr-bishop Ignatius of Antioch of the early second century summarizes for us the whole economy of our salvation.

Lord Jesus Christ,
on the human side you are sprung from David's
      line,
Son of God according to God's will and power,
born of the Virgin Mary, baptized by John,
and actually crucified for us in the flesh,
under Pontius Pilate and Herod the Tetrarch.
On the third day you raised a standard
to rally your saints and faithful for ever
in the one body of your Church.
By the grace and power of these mysteries,
fit us out with unshakable faith,
nail us body and soul to your cross,
and root us in love by your blood shed for us,
O Savior of the world,
living and reigning, now and for ever.
~AMEN.[10]

A Prayer of the Passion

In the last third of the second century a famous bishop, Melito of Sardis, summarized Christ's passion in full with affective piety.

Lord Jesus Christ,
you were bound as a ram,
you were shorn like a lamb,
you were led to the slaughter like a sheep,
you bore the wood of the cross on your shoulders,
you were led up the hill of Calvary,
you were displayed naked on the cross,
you were nailed to the bitter cross by three spikes,
you delivered your last seven words from the cross,
you died on the cross with a shout of victory,
you were buried in noble Joseph's rock-hewn tomb:
By your boundless suffering on our behalf,
fix our eyes unceasingly on your broken body
and the blood that poured from your hands, feet,
      and side.
By the holy sacrifice of the Mass
that renews each day your sacrifice
of the cross on our altars,
apply the merits of the cross to all humanity
and especially to those who worship it daily
and who offer themselves to you,
our great high priest and perpetual intercessor
before the eternal throne of God.

You live and reign through all the ages of ages.
~Amen.[11]

The Sufferings of Jesus

St. Thomas Aquinas, OP (ca. 1225–1274) details the various sufferings that Jesus endured during his sacred passion for us and for our salvation.

Christ suffered from friends abandoning him;
in his reputation from the blasphemies hurled at
      him;
in his honor and glory, from the mockeries and the
    insults heaped upon him;
in things, for he was despoiled of his garments;
in his soul, from sadness, weariness, and fear;
in his body, from wounds and scourgings.

In his head he suffered from the crown of piercing
      thorns;
in his hands and feet, from the fixing of the nails;
on his face from the blows and spittle;
from the lashes over his entire body.

He also suffered in all his bodily senses;
in touch, by being beaten and nailed to the cross;
in taste, by being given vinegar and gall to drink;
in smell, by being fastened to the gibbet in a place
    called Calvary, reeking with the stench of corpses;
in hearing, by being tormented with the cries of
      blasphemers and scorners;

in sight, by seeing the tears of his mother and of the disciple whom he loved.[12]

The Events before the Crucifixion

Eternal Wisdom speaks to Henry Suso:

Listen attentively to how intense was the suffering on your behalf. After the Last Supper . . . I surrendered myself to the throes of a cruel death and discovered that I was about to confront it; because of the fear in my gentle heart and the distress of my whole body, a bloody sweat began to pour out of me. I was treacherously taken captive, tightly bound and led off to agony. All through the night I was shamefully mistreated with blows, spat upon and blindfolded. In the morning, before Caiaphas, I was slandered and condemned to death. One could see the indescribable heartbreak of my pure Mother from the time she first saw me in distress until I was executed on the cross. I was brought before Pilate ignominiously, falsely accused and condemned to death. With their cruel eyes they stood opposite me, powerful as giants, and I stood before them like a gentle lamb. I, eternal Wisdom, was scorned as a fool in white garments before Herod. My fair body was torn open and marred by the wanton blows of the scourge. My gentle head was pierced and my loving countenance dripped with blood and spit. Thus was I condemned in misery and shamefully led forth with my cross to death. They screamed at me so cruelly that the air rang with their cries: "Crucify him! Crucify the evil fiend!"

Blessed Henry Suso, OP (1295–1366)[13]

His Sufferings

As the solemn days [of Holy Week] proceed, we shall be especially called on to consider His sufferings in the body, His seizure, His forced journeyings to and fro, His blows and wounds, His scourging, the crown of thorns, the nails, the Cross. They are all summed up in the Crucifix itself, as it meets our eyes; they are represented all at once on His sacred flesh, as it hangs before us—and meditation is made easy by the spectacle. It is otherwise with the sufferings of His soul; they cannot be painted for us, nor can they be duly investigated: they are beyond both sense and thought; and yet they anticipated His bodily sufferings. The agony, a pain of soul, not of the body, was the first act of His tremendous sacrifice; "My soul is sorrowful even unto death," He said; nay; if He suffered in the body, it really was in the soul, for the body did but convey the infliction on to that which was the true recipient and seat of the suffering.

Blessed John Henry Newman (1801–1890).[14]

The Five Hours of the Holy Cross: A Little Office of the Passion

After the Lord's Day, Friday was the next day of the week to be set aside for a special observance. As early as the second century, Friday became a weekly commemoration of the passion and death of our Savior and was observed by prayer and fasting. After the Empress Helena (ca. 250–330) discovered the True Cross, its title "Jesus of Nazareth, King of the Jews," and the nails, they were gradually distributed throughout the Catholic world. Devotion increased to these supreme relics of Jesus' passion and death, and the Office of the Cross became an important part of the emerging Books of Hours. Unfortunately, two of the most famous relics of the cross have been lost to wars and theft, but Rome still possesses and venerates a major piece of the cross and the Shroud of Turin. Some people will have the time to pray all five "hours" each day, others several, others only one "hour"; even one hour will give a taste of the cross.

> "See the glory of the Cross:
> the world was not subdued by iron weapons
> but by the wood of the Cross."
> **St. Augustine of Hippo Regius (354–430)**[15]

Mattins/Vigils: Grief in the Garden of Gethsemane

The three chosen disciples, Peter, James, and John, were with Jesus on the holy mountain when he was transfigured before them and revealed again as the Father's beloved Son. Now they are with him in his hour of agony. As he sweats like blood, however, they sleep! Judas gives him the kiss of death and the guards hustle Jesus away to the high priests, Annas and Caiaphas.

Jesus knew ✝ that his hour had come
~To go to his Father.
Even though I must die with you,
~I will not deny you, said Simon Peter.

Psalm 117   A Call to Praise and Prayer nab

The leader of prayer begins the Antiphon to the asterisk, and all continue it.

Antiphon Come, let us adore * the suffering servant of God.

Praise the Lord, all you nations!
  Give glory, all you peoples!
The Lord's love for us is strong;
  the Lord is faithful for ever.

Antiphon Come, let us adore the suffering servant of God.

Glory to the Father, and to the Son,
  and to the Holy Spirit:
as it was in the beginning, is now,
  and will be for ever. Amen.

Antiphon Come, let us adore the suffering servant of God.

A Hymn of the Passion

Go to dark Gethsemane,
You that feel the tempter's power;
Your Redeemer's conflict see,
Watch with him one bitter hour;
Turn not from his griefs away,
Learn of Jesus Christ to pray.

Follow to the judgment hall;
View the Lord of life arraigned;

O the wormwood and the gall!
O the pangs his soul sustained!
Shun not suffering, shame, or loss;
Learn from Christ to bear the cross.

Calvary's mournful mountain climb;
There, adoring at his feet,
Mark the miracle of time,
God's own sacrifice complete;
"It is finished!" hear him cry;
Learn from Jesus Christ to die.

James Montgomery (1771–1854)[16]

Psalm 41:1–2, 6–12   In Time of Betrayal

Antiphon O Lord, be gracious to me * and raise me up.

Blessed are those who consider the poor!
  The Lord delivers them in the day of trouble;
the Lord protects them and keeps them alive;
  they are called blessed in the land;
  you do not give them up to their enemies.

Those who come to see me utter empty words,
  while their hearts gather mischief;
  when they go out, they tell it abroad.
All who hate me whisper together about me;
  they imagine the worst for me,
  that I will not rise again from where I lie.
Even my bosom friend in whom I trusted,
  who ate of my bread, has lifted a heel against me.

ANTIPHON O LORD, BE GRACIOUS TO ME AND RAISE ME UP.

PSALM PRAYER

Let us pray (*pause for quiet prayer*):

Lord Jesus, man of sorrows,
in your prolonged agony in the garden,
you were deeply grieved, even to death,
and prayed that the cup of suffering
might pass you by.
May we, too, trust in Abba, your dear Father,
even when we are fearful,
but await in hope for the promised outcome.
Your reign is a reign for all ages.
~AMEN.

AFTER THE
1. READING   LAST SUPPER   MARK 14:26–31

When they had sung the hymn [Psalms 113–118],
they went out to the Mount of Olives. And Jesus
said to them, "You will all become deserters; for it
is written, 'I will strike the shepherd and the sheep
will be scattered.' But after I am raised up, I will
go before you to Galilee."

Peter said to him, "Even though all become
deserters, I will not." Jesus said to him, "Truly I tell
you, this day, this very night before the cock crows
twice, you will deny me three times." But he said

vehemently, "Even though I must die with you, I will not deny you." And all of them said the same.

Pause for quiet prayer

RESPONSORY

I will strike the shepherd
~I WILL STRIKE THE SHEPHERD

And the sheep will be scattered.
~I WILL STRIKE THE SHEPHERD

Glory to the Father, and to the Son,
  and to the Holy Spirit:
~I WILL STRIKE THE SHEPHERD.

THE AGONY IN
2. READING   **THE GARDEN**   **MARK 14:32–36**

Jesus and his disciples went to a place called Gethsemane; and he said to his disciples, "Sit here while I pray." He took with him Peter and James and John, and he began to be distressed and agitated. And he said to them, "I am deeply grieved, even to death; remain here, and keep awake." And going a little further, he threw himself on the ground and prayed that, if it were possible, the hour might pass from him. He said, "Abba, Father, for you all things are possible; remove this cup from me; yet not what I want, but what you want."

Pause for quiet prayer

Responsory

I am deeply grieved, even to death.

~I AM DEEPLY GRIEVED, EVEN TO DEATH.

Remain here, and stay awake with me.

~I AM DEEPLY GRIEVED, EVEN TO DEATH.

Glory to the Father, and to the Son,
  and to the Holy Spirit:

~I AM DEEPLY GRIEVED, EVEN TO DEATH.

A Canticle of Isaiah the Prophet 12:1–6

ANTIPHON Judas went up to Jesus and said, *
  "RABBI!" AND KISSED HIM.

You will say in that day:
I will give thanks to you, O LORD,
  for though you were angry with me,
your anger turned away,
  and comforted me.

Surely God is my salvation;
  I will trust, and will not be afraid,
for the LORD GOD is my strength and my might;
  for he has become my salvation.

Give thanks to the LORD,
  call on his name;
make known his deeds among the nations;
  proclaim that his name is exalted.

Sing praises to the LORD, for he has done
      gloriously;

let this be known in all the earth.
Shout aloud and sing for joy, O royal Zion,
    for great in your midst is the Holy One of Israel

Glory to the Holy and Undivided Trinity:
now and always and for ever and ever. Amen.

ANTIPHON JUDAS WENT UP TO JESUS AND SAID,
    "RABBI!" AND KISSED HIM.

A LITANY OF THE PASSION

Lord Jesus, in the garden of Gethsemane,
        you offered up prayers and tears to God:
~SAVE US FROM DEATH.

Lord Jesus, you prayed in great agony and distress
        to your Abba:
~SAVE US FROM DEATH.

Lord Jesus, your sweat became like great drops
        of blood falling to the ground:
~SAVE US FROM DEATH.

Lord Jesus, you were greatly grieved even to death:
~SAVE US FROM DEATH.

Lord Jesus, you were betrayed by Judas with a kiss:
~SAVE US FROM DEATH.

Lord Jesus, you were deserted by all your disciples:
~SAVE US FROM DEATH.

Lord Jesus, you were arrested, bound, and taken
        before the high priests, Annas and Caiaphas:
~SAVE US FROM DEATH.

Lord Jesus, you were denied by Simon Peter three
times
before cockcrow:
~SAVE US FROM DEATH.

Pause for our special intentions.

Lord Jesus, by the prayers of Our Lady of Mercy
who stood at the foot of the cross,
with the other women, and the beloved
disciple:
~SAVE US FROM DEATH.

CLOSING PRAYER
Jesus, Savior,
even though you trust your dear Father,
as your hour of death approaches,
you fall into fear and trembling
at the vision of your dreadful dying.
Be with us, Lord, in the time of trial,
deliver us from our doubts and fears,
and make us trust completely
in your saving cross.
You live and reign with the Father,
in the unity of the Holy Spirit,
one God, for ever and ever.
~AMEN.

With joy you will draw water
~FROM THE WELLS OF SALVATION.

BLESSING

May the glorious passion of our Lord Jesus Christ
✝ bring us to the joys of paradise.
~AMEN.

Morning Praise/Lauds: Four Trials

After the scenes in the garden, we now consider the four "trials" that Jesus undergoes before the two high priests, Annas and Caiaphas, and then before Herod and Pontius Pilate the governor. Annas asks questions out of curiosity and Jesus has to endure a blow to the face for a remark to a guard; Caiaphas presides over an actual trial for blasphemy and condemns Jesus insofar as he can go; the puppet King Herod amuses himself with Jesus and then returns him to Pilate and the death sentence.

O God, ✝ come to my assistance;
~O LORD, MAKE HASTE TO HELP ME.

The wicked prowl on every side
~WHEN VILENESS IS EXALTED AMONG
      HUMANKIND.

A HYMN OF THE PASSION

O love, how deep, how broad, how high,
How passing thought and fantasy,
That God, the Son of God should take
Our mortal form for mortals' sake.

For us to evil power betrayed,
Scourged, mocked, in purple robe arrayed,

He bore the shameful cross and death,
For us gave up his dying breath.

For us he rose from death again;
For us he went on high to reign;
For us he sent the Spirit here
To guide, to strengthen, and to cheer.

All glory to our Lord and God
For love so deep, so high, so broad:
The Trinity whom we adore
Forever and forevermore.[17]

PSALM 12   CHRIST PRAYS FOR HELP

The leader of prayer begins the Antiphon to the asterisk and all continue it.

The leader prays the stanzas of the psalm and all repeat the Antiphon.

ANTIPHON The wicked have gathered together *
AGAINST THE LORD AND HIS ANOINTED.

Help, O Lord; no one who is godly is left,
    for the faithful have vanished from humankind.
They utter lies to one another;
    they speak with flattering lips and a double heart.

May the Lord cut off flattering lips,
    the tongue that makes great boasts,
those who say, "With our tongues we will prevail,
    our lips are our own; who is our master?"

The Lord says, "Now I will arise,
  because the poor are plundered,
  because the needy groan;
  I will place them in the safety
    for which they long."

The promises of the Lord are promises
    that are pure,
  silver refined in an earthen furnace,
  purified seven times.

Protect us, O Lord;
  guard us from this generation forever.
The wicked prowl on every side
  when vileness is exalted among humankind.

ANTIPHON THE WICKED HAVE GATHERED TOGETHER
  AGAINST THE LORD AND HIS ANOINTED.

PSALM PRAYER
Let us pray (*pause for quiet prayer*):

Righteous God,
your dear Son cried out to you
against his many false accusers
but kept silence before them.
For the sake of Jesus,
rescue us from resentment
and the desire for vindication;
now and for ever.
~AMEN.

They took Jesus to the high priest; and all the chief priests, the elders, and the scribes were assembled. Now the chief priests were looking for testimony against Jesus to put him to death; but they found none. For many gave false testimony, and their testimony did not agree. Some stood up and gave false testimony against him, saying, "We heard him say, 'I will destroy this temple that is made with hands, and in three days I will build another, not made with hands.'" But even on this point their testimony did not agree. Then the high priest stood up before them and asked Jesus, "Have you no answer? What is it that they testify against you?" But he was silent and did not answer. Again the high priest asked him, "Are you the Messiah, the Son of the Blessed One?" Jesus said, "I am; and

> 'you will see the Son of Man
> seated at the right hand of the Power,'
> and 'coming with the clouds of heaven.'"

Then the high priest tore his clothes and said, "Why do we still need witnesses? You have heard his blasphemy! What is your decision?" All of them condemned him as deserving death. Some began to spit on him, to blindfold him, and to strike him, saying to him, "Prophesy!" The guards also took him over and beat him.

Pause for quiet prayer

RESPONSORY

Although he was a Son, he learned obedience
through what he suffered.

~ALTHOUGH HE WAS A SON, HE LEARNED
OBEDIENCE THROUGH WHAT HE SUFFERED.

A broken and contrite heart, O God, you will not
despise.

~ALTHOUGH HE WAS A SON, HE LEARNED
OBEDIENCE THROUGH WHAT HE SUFFERED.

Glory to the Father, and to the Son,
and to the Holy Spirit:

~ALTHOUGH HE WAS A SON, HE LEARNED
OBEDIENCE THROUGH WHAT HE SUFFERED.

2. READING   **BEFORE PONTIUS PILATE**   **JOHN 18:33–40; 19:1**

Pilate summoned Jesus and asked him, "Are you the King of the Jews?" Jesus answered, "Do you ask this on your own, or did others tell you about me?" Pilate replied, "I am not a Jew, am I? Your own nation and the chief priests have handed you over to me. What have you done?" Jesus answered, "My kingdom is not from this world. If my kingdom were from this world, my followers would be fighting to keep me from being handed over to the Jews. But, as it is, my kingdom is not from here." Pilate asked him, "So you are a king?" Jesus answered, "You say that I am a king. For this I was born, and for this I came into the world, to testify to the truth. Every one who belongs to the truth listens to my voice." Pilate asked him, "What is truth?" After he had said this he went out to the Jews again and told them, "I find no case against him. But you have a custom that I release someone for you at the Passover. Do you want me to release for you the King of the Jews?" They shouted in reply, "Not this man, but Barabbas!" Now Barabbas was a bandit. Then Pilate took Jesus and had him flogged.

Pause for quiet prayer

RESPONSORY

Jesus was a man of suffering and acquainted
    with infirmity.

~JESUS WAS A MAN OF SUFFERING AND
    ACQUAINTED WITH INFIRMITY.

"I find no case in him," said Pontius Pilate.

~JESUS WAS A MAN OF SUFFERING AND
    ACQUAINTED WITH INFIRMITY.

Glory to the Father, and to the Son,
    and to the Holy Spirit:

~JESUS WAS A MAN OF SUFFERING AND
    ACQUAINTED WITH INFIRMITY.

A Canticle of Isaiah the Prophet 5:1–6 — God's Vineyard

Antiphon Let me sing for my beloved *
  MY LOVE-SONG CONCERNING HIS VINEYARD:

My beloved had a vineyard
  on a very fertile hill.
He dug it and cleared it of stones,
  and planted it with choice vines;
he built a watchtower in the midst of it,
  and hewed out a wine vat in it;
he expected it to yield grapes,
  but it yielded sour grapes.

And now, inhabitants of Jerusalem,
  and people of Judah,
judge between me
  and my vineyard.
What more was there to do for my vineyard
  that I have not done in it?
When I expected it to yield grapes,
  why did it yield sour grapes?

And now I will tell you
  what I will do to my vineyard.
I will remove its hedge,
  and it shall be devoured;
I will break down its wall,
  and it shall be trampled down.

I will make it a waste;
  it shall not be pruned or hoed,
  and it shall be overgrown
    with briers and thorns;
I will also command the clouds
  that they rain no rain upon it.

Glory to the Holy and Undivided Trinity:
  now and always and for ever and ever. Amen.

ANTIPHON LET ME SING FOR MY BELOVED
  MY LOVE-SONG CONCERNING MY VINEYARD.

A LITANY OF THE PASSION

Lord Jesus, man of sorrows, the priests and
  elders of Israel conspired against you:
~SAVE US FROM THE TIME OF TRIAL.

Lord Jesus, the high priest Annas questioned you
  about your disciples and your teaching:
~SAVE US FROM THE TIME OF TRIAL.

Lord Jesus, the high priest Caiaphas looked for
  false testimony against you:
~SAVE US FROM THE TIME OF TRIAL.

Lord Jesus, Caiaphas accused you of blasphemy
  and found you worthy of death:
~SAVE US FROM THE TIME OF TRIAL.

Lord Jesus, Herod and his soldiers treated you
  with contempt and mockery:
~SAVE US FROM THE TIME OF TRIAL.

Lord Jesus, Pontius Pilate found no case against
     you but the crowd demanded your death
     sentence:
~Save us from the time of trial.

Lord Jesus, Pilate released Barabbas who the
     crowd asked for and handed you over to
     crucifixion:
~Save us from the time of trial.

Pause for our special intentions.

Lord Jesus, by the prayers of your sorrowful
     Mother and of all the saints in glory:
~Save us from the time of trial.

The Lord's Prayer
Lord, have mercy.
~Christ, have mercy. Lord, have mercy.

Our Father in heaven, (all in unison):

Closing Prayer
Before priests and princes, good Lord,
you were slandered and falsely accused
by those intent on your death:
By your holy innocence,
please protect us from the violent,
and from those who set snares for us.
Your reign is a reign for all ages.
~Amen.

You will see the Son of Man
~Coming with the clouds of heaven..

Doxology
To the One seated on the throne and to the Lamb
be blessing and honor and glory and might
for ever and ever.
~Amen.

Noonday: Jesus Is Scourged and Crowned with Thorns

Pontius Pilate ordered Jesus to be flogged almost to death and then allowed him to be mocked and ridiculed by his whole cohort of cruel soldiers as they both spat on him and hailed him as the King of the Jews. Jesus was dressed in a purple robe of mockery, crowned with a piercing helmet of thorns, and given a mock scepter of reeds to demonstrate his weakened state.

> "Sweet Jesus, your body is like a book written all over with red ink."
>
> **Richard Rolle of Hampole (ca. 1300–1349)**[18]

Be pleased, **†** O God, to deliver me!
~O Lord, make haste to help me!
But I am poor and needy;
~Hasten to help me, O God!

A Hymn of the Passion

Jesus, when faith with constant eyes
Regards your wondrous sacrifice,
Love rises to an ardent flame,
And we all other hope disclaim.

With cold affection who can see
The lash, the thorns, the nails, the tree,
The flowing tears and purple sweat,
The bleeding hands, and head, and feet.

Look saints, into his gaping side,
The cleft how large, how deep, how wide?
There issues forth a double flood
Of cleansing water, pardoning blood.

From there, O soul, a balsam flows
To heal your wounds, and cure your woes;
Immortal joys come streaming down,
Joys, like his griefs, immense, unknown.

Thus I could ever, ever sing
The sufferings of my heavenly King;
With growing pleasure spread abroad
The mysteries of a dying god.

John Rippon (1751–1836)[19]

Psalm 142   Jesus Cries Out to His Father

Antiphon Bring me out of prison, O God, *
 so that I may give thanks to your name!

With my voice I cry to the Lord,

I make supplication;
before the Lord I tell my trouble,
  I pour out my complaint.
When my spirit is faint,
  you know my way.

In the path where I walk
  they have hidden a trap for me.
Look on my right hand and see;
  there is no one who takes notice of me;
no refuge remains for me;
  no one cares for me.

I cry to you, O Lord;
  I say, "You are my refuge,
  my portion in the land of the living."
Give heed to my cry;
  for I am brought very low.
Save me from my persecutors;
  for they are too strong for me.
Bring me out of prison,
  so that I may give thanks to your name!
The righteous will surround me,
  for you will deal richly with me.

ANTIPHON BRING ME OUT OF PRISON, O GOD,
    SO THAT I MAY GIVE THANKS TO YOUR NAME!

PSALM PRAYER
Let us pray (*pause for quiet prayer*):

Crucified Savior,
your Holy Father permitted Pontius Pilate
to have you flogged and mocked
and sent to the cross.
And yet he, your Abba, brought you out
    of the prison of death
and dealt richly with you.
Help us in our hour of need
and by the blood you shed for us
deliver us from all sin and error.
You live and reign, now and for ever.
~Amen.

1. A Reading on the Mockery of Jesus   John 19:2–6

The solders wove a crown of thorns and put it on
his head, and dressed him in a purple robe. They
kept coming up to him, saying, "Hail, King of the
Jews!" and striking him on the face. Pilate went
out again and said to them, "Look, I am bringing
him out to you to let you know that I find no
case against him." So Jesus came out, wearing the
crown of thorns and the purple robe. Pilate said to
them, "Here is the man!" When the chief priests
and the police saw him, they shouted, "Crucify
him! Crucify him!"

Pause for quiet prayer

RESPONSORY

The soldiers began saluting Jesus.

~THE SOLDIERS BEGAN SALUTING JESUS.

"Hail, King of the Jews."

~THE SOLDIERS BEGAN SALUTING JESUS.

Glory to the Father, and to the Son,
and to the Holy Spirit:

~THE SOLDIERS BEGAN SALUTING JESUS.

2. A READING OF JULIAN OF NORWICH ON THE CROWN OF THORNS

"Now at once I saw the red blood trickling down
from under the garland. Hot and freely it fell,
copious and real it was, as if it had just been
pressed down upon his blessed head, who is truly
both God and man, the very same that suffered
thus for me. . . . Yet in this sight of his blessed
passion and the Godhead that I saw with my full
understanding. I knew well that it was strength
enough for me (and for that matter all who are
saved) to withstand all the fiends of hell and any
other ghostly temptation."

Blessed Julian of Norwich (ca. 1342–1423)[20]

Pause for quiet prayer

RESPONSORY

Without the shedding of blood,

~WITHOUT THE SHEDDING OF BLOOD.

There is no forgiveness of sins,
~WITHOUT THE SHEDDING OF BLOOD.

Glory to the Father, and to the Son,
and to the Holy Spirit:
~WITHOUT THE SHEDDING OF BLOOD.

A CANTICLE OF THE LAMB OF GOD
REVELATION 4:11; 5:9–10, 12

ANTIPHON Help your people, Lord, *
BOUGHT WITH THE PRICE OF YOUR OWN BLOOD.

You are worthy, our Lord and God,
to receive glory and honor and power,
for you created all things,
and by your will they existed and were created.

You are worthy, O Christ,
to take the scroll and to open its seals,
for you were slaughtered
and by your blood you ransomed for God
saints from every tribe and language
and people and nation;
and have made them to be a kingdom and priests
serving our God,
and they will reign on earth.

Worthy is the Lamb that was slaughtered
to receive power and wealth and wisdom
and might and honor and glory and blessing!

ANTIPHON HELP YOUR PEOPLE, LORD,
BOUGHT WITH THE PRICE OF YOUR OWN BLOOD.

CLOSING PRAYER

Abba, dear Father,
look upon this family of yours
for which our Lord Jesus Christ
did not hesitate to hand himself over to sinners
and undergo the torment of the cross.
He lives and reigns with you, in the unity of the
Holy Spirit,
one God, for ever and ever.
~AMEN.

The sign of the cross will appear in the heavens
~WHEN THE LORD JESUS RETURNS IN GLORY!

BLESSING

By his holy and glorious wounds
may Christ Jesus ✝ protect us and keep us.
~AMEN.

Evensong/Vespers: Jesus Walks the Way of the Cross

The way of the cross from Pilate's court to Calvary was the bitter prelude to the actual crucifixion of Jesus. The priests and the crowds shouted for his death, Pilate sentenced him to crucifixion, Simon of Cyrene came to his assistance, the wailing women lamented his pitiful state, and the Roman guards nailed him to the cross.

The Signs of Love

Once during Lent great desire and power-ful grace were given me to serve God more perfectly. I felt how our Lord's works of love increased powerfully in me. And I desired that my whole body would be full of the signs of love of the holy cross, as many as possible to be on me, and that each one would be given to me with all its suffering and pain over my entire body.

Blessed Margaret Ebner, OP (1291–1351)[21]

Pilate handed Jesus ✝ over to be crucified.
~HE WAS LED LIKE A LAMB TO THE SLAUGHTER.
Blest be Simon of Cyrene,
~WHO CARRIED THE CROSS BEHIND JESUS.

HYMN

Lord Jesus, at this hour you took
The cross on which you conquered death;
You took the way that led to life,
The Spirit's gift your dying breath.

Almighty Father, at this hour
You sent the spirit of your Son
To bring true peace to all the earth,
And make your scattered children one.

God's promised Gift, you came to warm
Our lukewarm hearts with living fire;
Bring now to life a lifeless world,
And loveless hearts with love inspire.

Praise God the Father, gracious Lord,
Praise God, his dear and only Son,
Praise God the Spirit, bond of love,
Praise God, who is for ever one.

James Quinn, SJ[22]

PSALM 22:1–2, 6–8, 14–20   JESUS CRIES OUT TO HIS FATHER

ANTIPHON They tear holes in my hands and my
feet * AND LAY ME IN THE DUST OF DEATH.

My God, my God, why have you forsaken me?
  Why are you so far from helping me,
  from the words of my groaning?

O my God, I cry by day, but you do not answer;
  and by night, but find no rest.
Yet you, the praise of Israel,
  are enthroned in holiness.

But I am a worm, not human;
  scorned by others, and despised by the people.
All who see me mock at me,
  they make mouths at me, they wag their heads
      and say:

"You committed your cause to the Lord;
  let the Lord deliver you.
  Let the Lord rescue you,
  for the Lord delights in you!"

I am poured out like water,
  and all my bones are out of joint;
my heart is like wax,
  melted within my breast;
my mouth is dried up like a potsherd,
  and my tongue sticks to my jaws;
  you lay me in the dust of death.

Indeed, dogs surround me;
  a company of evildoers encircles me;
  my hands and feet are bound.
I can count all my bones;
  they stare and gloat over me;
They divide my garments among them,
  and cast lots for my clothing.

But you, O Lord, be not far away!
  O my help, hasten to my aid!
Deliver my soul from the sword,
  my life from the power of the dog!

Antiphon They tear holes in my hands and
    my feet and lay me in the dust of death.

Psalm Prayer

Let us pray (*pause for quiet prayer*):

Lord Jesus Crucified,
your five priceless wounds
are indelible marks of love made visible:
On the cross of pain,

you begged your Father for help
and he rescued you from death and the grave
and raised you into glory.
Come now to our assistance
in our hour of need
and be our precious Savior.
Blest be the holy name of Jesus.
~AMEN.

1. READING   BLOOD ON US   MATTHEW 27:24–26

So when Pilate saw that he could do nothing, but
rather that a riot was beginning, he took some
water and washed his hands before the crowd,
saying, "I am innocent of this man's blood; see to it
yourselves." Then the people as a whole answered,
"His blood be on us and on our children." So he
released Barabbas for them; and after flogging
Jesus, he handed him over to be crucified.

Pause for quiet prayer

RESPONSORY

I am innocent of this man's blood.
~I AM INNOCENT OF THIS MAN'S BLOOD.

See to it yourselves.
~I AM INNOCENT OF THIS MAN'S BLOOD.

Glory to the Father, and to the Son,
  and to the Holy Spirit:
~I AM INNOCENT OF THIS MAN'S BLOOD.

2. READING   SIMON AND THE WOMEN   LUKE 23:26–31

As they led him away, they seized a man, Simon of Cyrene, who was coming from the country, and they laid the cross on him, and made him carry it behind Jesus. A great number of the people followed him, and among them were women who were beating their breasts and wailing for him. But Jesus turned to them and said, "Daughters of Jerusalem, do not weep for me, but weep for yourselves and for your children. For the days are surely coming when they will say, 'Blessed are the barren, and the wombs that never bore, and the breasts that never nursed.' Then they will begin to say to the mountains, 'Fall on us'; and to the hills, 'Cover us.' For if they do this when the wood is green, what will happen when it is dry?"

Pause for quiet prayer

RESPONSORY

Jesus suffered under Pontius Pilate.

~JESUS SUFFERED UNDER PONTIUS PILATE;

He was crucified, died, and was buried.

~JESUS SUFFERED UNDER PONTIUS PILATE;

Glory to the Father, and to the Son,
  and to the Holy Spirit:

~JESUS SUFFERED UNDER PONTIUS PILATE.

A CANTICLE OF THE PROPHET JONAH   2:2–7 TEV

ANTIPHON From deep in the world of the dead *
   I CRIED FOR HELP AND YOU HEARD ME.

In my distress, O Lord, I called to you,
  and you answered me.
From deep in the world of the dead
  I cried for help and you heard me.

You threw me down into the depths,
  to the very bottom of the sea,
  where the waters were all around me,
  and all your mighty waves rolled over me.
I thought I had been banished from your presence
  and would never see your holy Temple again.

The water came over me and choked me;
  the sea covered me completely,
  and seaweed wrapped around my head.
I went down to the very roots of the mountains,
  into the land whose gates lock shut for ever.

But you, O Lord my God,
  brought me back from the depths alive.
When I felt my life slipping away,
  then, O Lord, I prayed to you,
  and in your holy Temple you heard me.

Glory to the Holy and Undivided Trinity:
  now and always and for ever and ever.
~AMEN.

ANTIPHON FROM DEEP IN THE WORLD OF THE DEAD
I CRIED FOR HELP AND YOU HEARD ME.

A LITANY OF THE CROSS

Let us thank Jesus for his torn back
  from the Roman scourge:
~THANK YOU, LORD JESUS.

Let us thank him for his bloodied head
  and shoulders from the crown of thorns:
~THANK YOU, LORD JESUS.

Let us thank Jesus for his five wounds,
  like five rubies in his flesh:
~THANK YOU, LORD JESUS.

Let us thank Jesus for forgiving his enemies
  from the cross:
~THANK YOU, LORD JESUS.

Let us thank Jesus for his deadly thirst
  on the cross:
~THANK YOU, LORD JESUS.

Let us thank Jesus for commending his spirit
  to his Father as he died on the cross:
~THANK YOU, LORD JESUS.

Let us thank Jesus for pouring out blood and
          water
  from his side after his death:
~THANK YOU, LORD JESUS.

Pause for our special intentions.

Let us thank Jesus for his sorrowful Mother
  standing near his cross and for the other
      mourners:
~Thank you, Lord Jesus.

Closing Prayer

Lord Jesus, suffering servant of God,
you were born for us in the poverty of Bethlehem
and died for us on the bitter hill of Calvary.
By the blessed crib and the awesome cross,
lift our hearts to your dazzling resurrection,
O Lord of Glory,
living and reigning with the Father,
in the unity of the Holy Spirit,
now and for ever.
~Amen.

Glory and power to the victorious cross,
~The price of our salvation.

May the glorious passion of our Lord Jesus Christ
✝ bring us to the joys of paradise.
~Amen.

Night Prayer/Compline

Crucifixion leads to death, to the taking him down from
the cross, to the laying him in his mother's arms, to his
wrapping in the holy shroud, to his laying in the fresh-
cut tomb, to the rolling door shut to the tomb; and the
departure of the eyewitnesses.

Jesus ✝ is the Good Shepherd, who was willing
~To lay down his life for the sheep.
Mary's canticle puts an end
~to the lamentations of Eve.

Hymn

O Cross of Christ, immortal tree
On which our Savior died,
The world is sheltered by your arms
That bore the Crucified.

From bitter death and barren wood
The tree of life is made;
Its branches bear unfailing fruit
And leaves that never fade.

O faithful Cross, you stand unmoved
While ages run their course;
Foundation of the universe,
Creation's binding force.

Give glory to the risen Christ
And to his Cross give praise,
The sign of God's unfathomed love,
The hope of all our days.[23]

Wisdom 2:12–20   Jesus Crucified

Antiphon Let us test him with insult and torture, *
and condemn him to a shameful death.

"Let us lie in wait for the righteous man,
because he is inconvenient to us

and opposes our actions;
he reproaches us for sins against the law,
and accuses us of sins against our training.
He professes to have knowledge of God,
and calls himself a child of the Lord.

He became to us a reproof of our thoughts;
the very sight of him is a burden to us,
because his manner of life is unlike that of others,
and his ways are strange.

We are considered by him as something base,
and he avoids our ways as unclean;
he calls the last end of the righteous happy,
and boasts that God is his father.

Let us see if his words are true,
and let us test what will happen
    at the end of his life;
for if the righteous man is God's child,
    he will help him,
and will deliver him from the hand
    of his adversaries.

Let us test him with insult and torture,
so that we might find out how gentle he is,
and make trial of his forbearance.
Let us condemn him to a shameful death,
for, according to what he says,
    he will be protected.

ANTIPHON LET US TEST HIM WITH INSULT AND
TORTURE AND CONDEMN HIM TO A SHAMEFUL
DEATH.

PRAYER

Let us pray (*pause for quiet prayer*):

Father of Jesus,
your dear Child has full knowledge of you,
calls himself your true Son,
and whose manner of life is unlike that
    of other people:
Be with us in the person of Jesus,
do not forsake us in the time of trial
or at the hour of our death.
Blessed be his holy Name, now and for ever!
~AMEN.

1. READING   NAILED TO THE CROSS   JOHN 19:16–19, 23–15

Pilate handed over Jesus to them to be crucified. So
they took Jesus; and carrying the cross by himself,
he went out to what is called the Place of the Skull.
There they crucified him, and with him two others,
one on either side, with Jesus between them. Pilate
also had an inscription written and put on the cross.
It read, "Jesus of Nazareth, the King of the Jews."

When the soldiers had crucified Jesus, they
took his clothes and divided them into four parts,
one for each soldier. They also took his tunic; now

the tunic was seamless, woven in one piece from the top. So they said to one another, "Let us not tear it, but cast lots for it to see who will get it."

This was to fulfill what the scripture says,

"They divided my clothes among themselves,
and for my clothing they cast lots."

And that is what the soldiers did.

Pause for quiet prayer

Responsory

Jesus bore our sins in his body on the cross.

~JESUS BORE OUR SINS IN HIS BODY ON THE CROSS.

By his wounds we have been healed.

~JESUS BORE OUR SINS IN HIS BODY ON THE CROSS.

Glory to the Father, and to the Son,
   and to the Holy Spirit:

~JESUS BORE OUR SINS IN HIS BODY ON THE CROSS.

2. Reading   **His Last Breath**   **Matthew 27:50–54**

Jesus cried out with a loud voice and breathed his last. At that moment the curtain of the temple was torn in two, from top to bottom. The earth shook, and the rocks were split. The tombs also were opened, and many bodies of the saints who had fallen asleep were raised. After his resurrection they came out of the tombs and entered the holy city and appeared to many. Now when the centurion and those who were with him, who were keeping watch over Jesus, saw the earthquake and what took place, they were terrified and said, "Truly this man was God's Son!"

Pause for quiet prayer

RESPONSORY

Jesus bowed his head and gave up his spirit.
~JESUS BOWED HIS HEAD AND GAVE UP HIS SPIRIT.

The cross of Jesus is the life of the world.
~JESUS BOWED HIS HEAD AND GAVE UP HIS SPIRIT.

Glory to the Father, and to the Son,
   and to the Holy Spirit:
~JESUS BOWED HIS HEAD AND GAVE UP HIS SPIRIT.

A CANTICLE OF
ST. PAUL THE APOSTLE   PHILIPPIANS 2:5–11

ANTIPHON There is no other name under heaven *
   BY WHICH WE MUST BE SAVED.

Though Christ was in the form of God
he did not regard equality with God
as something to be exploited,
but emptied himself,
taking the form of a slave.
being born in human likeness.

And being found in human form,
he humbled himself
and became obedient to the point of death—

even death on a cross.

Therefore God also highly exalted him
and gave him the name
that is above every name,
so that at the name of Jesus
every knee should bend,
in heaven and on earth and under the earth,
and every tongue should confess
that Jesus Christ is Lord,
to the glory of God the Father.

ANTIPHON THERE IS NO OTHER NAME UNDER
HEAVEN BY WHICH WE MUST BE SAVED.

A LITANY OF THE CROSS

Lord Jesus, you embraced your bitter passion
and your dreadful death on the cross for us:
~LORD, HAVE MERCY.

Lord Jesus, you were fastened with nails
to the cruel wood of the cross:
~LORD, HAVE MERCY.

Lord Jesus, as you hung on the cross
you were taunted and derided
by priests, criminals, and soldiers:
~LORD, HAVE MERCY.

Lord Jesus, you forgave your enemies
from the cross:
~LORD, HAVE MERCY.

Lord Jesus, you promised Paradise
  to a repentant criminal:
~LORD, HAVE MERCY.

Lord Jesus, from the cross you confided
  your sorrowful Mother to your beloved disciple:
~LORD, HAVE MERCY.

Lord Jesus, you called out in agony at the ninth hour
  and died with a great cry:
~LORD, HAVE MERCY.

Lord Jesus, you were taken down from the cross
  and laid in your mother's arms:
~LORD, HAVE MERCY.

We pray for our special intentions.

Lord Jesus, you conquered death by your death
  and brought life to those in the grave:
~LORD, HAVE MERCY.

CLOSING PRAYER
Holy and compassionate Father,
on Good Friday afternoon,
your dear Son, our Savior,
spread out his hands to you
and to the whole world.
By the blood that issued from
  his five precious wounds,
wash away our sins,

fill us with his Holy Spirit,
and conduct us into the Paradise
    for ever green.
We ask this through Christ our Lord.
~Amen.

We adore you, O Christ, and we bless you;
~For by your holy cross you have redeemed
    the world.

May the glorious passion of our Lord Jesus Christ
✝ bring us to the joys of paradise.
~Amen.

Salve Regina
Hail, holy Queen, Mother of mercy, *
hail, our life, our sweetness, and our hope.
To you we cry, the children of Eve;
to you we send up our sighs,
mourning and weeping in this land of exile.
Turn, then, most gracious advocate,
your eyes of mercy toward us;
lead us home at last
and show us the blessed fruit of your womb,
        Jesus:
O clement, O loving, O sweet Virgin Mary.[24]

A Devotion to the Paschal Mystery

The true suffering servant of God foreshadowed in the Prophet Isaiah (42:1–4; 49:1–6; 50:4–11; 52:13—53:12) is Christ Jesus who "overcame the sting of death and opened the kingdom of heaven to all believers" (*Te Deum*). But his sufferings only preceded his glorious resurrection, his wonderful ascension, and his gift of the Spirit on Pentecost.

Lord Jesus, suffering servant of God,
you came into the world of sin and pain
to rescue us from our sorry situation,
and make us the children of God.
~GLORY TO YOU, O LORD, GLORY TO YOU!

Lord Jesus, suffering servant of God,
you entered into the final days of your life
to accomplish the loving will of God
by laying down your life for your friends.
~GLORY TO YOU, O LORD, GLORY TO YOU!

Lord Jesus, suffering servant of God,
you became the bread of life for us,
giving us your true flesh for our food
and your true blood for our drink.
~GLORY TO YOU, O LORD, GLORY TO YOU!

Lord Jesus, suffering servant of God,
you were betrayed by Judas with a kiss,
deserted by your chosen friends,
and denied three times by Simon Peter.
~GLORY TO YOU, O LORD, GLORY TO YOU!

Lord Jesus, suffering servant of God,
you were tried by faithless priests and elders,
manhandled, mocked, slapped, and spat upon,
accused of blasphemy, and accounted worthy of
      death.
~GLORY TO YOU, O LORD, GLORY TO YOU!

> Come, kneel before the Lord:
> He shed for us his blood;
> He died the victim of pure love
> To make us one with God.
> **Edward Caswall (1814–1878)**[25]

Lord Jesus, suffering servant of God,
you were handed over to Pontius Pilate,
denounced by many false witnesses,
while standing silent before your accusers.
~GLORY TO YOU, O LORD, GLORY TO YOU!

Lord Jesus, suffering servant of God,
you were condemned to a pitiless flagellation,
to the pain and humiliation of a mock coronation,
and the carrying of the cross to Golgotha.
~GLORY TO YOU, O LORD, GLORY TO YOU!

Lord Jesus, suffering servant of God,
you were nailed with three spikes to the cross,
taunted and jeered at by priests and criminals,
but attended by the three Marys and John,
    the beloved disciple.
~GLORY TO YOU, O LORD, GLORY TO YOU!

Lord Jesus, suffering servant of God,
you endured long hours on the cross,
asked forgiveness for all your enemies,
commended your spirit to your Father,
bowed your head, and breathed your last.
~Glory to you, O Lord, Glory to you!

Lord Jesus, suffering servant of God,
after your death you were pierced by a Roman spear,
poured forth blood and water for our salvation,
were taken down from the cross,
and laid in your dear mother's arms.
~Glory to you, O Lord, Glory to you!

> For us to evil power betrayed,
> Scourged, mocked, in purple robe arrayed,
> He bore the shameful cross and death,
> For us gave up his dying breath.
>
> **Thomas à Kempis**[26]

Lord Jesus, suffering servant of God,
as holy women from Galilee looked on,
noble Joseph wrapped you in a linen shroud,
laid you in his own new tomb hewn in the rock,
and rolled a great stone to the door of the tomb.
~Glory to you, O Lord, Glory to you!

Lord Jesus, suffering servant of God,
you broke open the gates of death,
descended among the righteous dead,

and brought life to those in the graves.
~GLORY TO YOU, O LORD, GLORY TO YOU!

Lord Jesus, suffering servant of God,
you rose from the dead on the third day,
appeared again and again for forty days,
speaking of the kingdom of God.
~GLORY TO YOU, O LORD, GLORY TO YOU!

Lord Jesus, suffering servant of God,
you took your place at God's right hand
in the midst of rejoicing saints and angels,
and now display your five wounds for us
before our dear Father for ever and ever.
~GLORY TO YOU, O LORD, GLORY TO YOU!

Lord Jesus, suffering servant of God,
victorious over sin and death and hell,
coming to judge the living and the dead,
and reigning in great power and glory,
    for ever and ever. Amen!
~GLORY TO YOU, O LORD, GLORY TO YOU!

> Christ the Victor over death,
> Breathe on us the Spirit's breath!
> Paradise is our reward,
> Endless Easter with our Lord!

James Quinn, SJ[27]

Let us pray:
God our Father,
you gave joy to the world

by the resurrection of your Son,
  our Lord Jesus Christ.
Through the prayers of his Mother,
  the Virgin Mary,
bring us to the happiness of eternal life.
We ask this through Christ our Lord.
~Amen.

The Face of God in Christ

God appeared in many ways and in many places in the long history of his chosen people Israel, but the Lord never allowed them to see his face because it was impossible for humans to bear its radiance and still live (Exodus 3:6; 24:15–18; 33:19–23; 34:29–35). But in the incarnation of the Word of God the face of God was revealed, uncovered in Jesus of Nazareth.

His disciples could watch him from day to day and discover what God was like; how he spoke, how he patiently explained his mission and vocation, how he ate and slept, how he put up with rejection and humiliation, how he cherished his friends, how he forgave his enemies, how he suffered and died on the cross, and, finally, how he appeared to his disciples after his resurrection "during forty days and speaking about the kingdom of God" (Acts 1:3).

Jesus is God at work in the world and when we seek his face we must find him in the Holy Gospels, on the cross, in the divine tradition of the Church, in the Blessed Sacrament of the Altar, in the lives of the saints, and in the lives of all the good Christians everywhere.

A Devotion to the Holy Face of Jesus

The English mystic Julian of Norwich (ca. 1342–1423) allows us to visualize the sufferings of Jesus in a way that permits us to see his blessed face and feel the suffering he endured for us.

Christ showed me part of his Passion near to his death. I saw his sweet face as it was then, all dry and bloodless with the pallor of dying, and by degrees grew even still more pale, dead and listless; and then as it became more lifeless, turning to blue. After this as death itself approached, the flesh turned from blue to brown. His passion was shown to me in his face, and in particular in his lips; where before they were fresh and ruddy and pleasing in my sight, I now saw only these four colors. It was distressing to see the change wrought in this deep dying; for instance, I noticed the nose was clogged and dried, and the sweet body was brown and black, quite bled of his own fair, lively color by this dry dying. For at the time our Lord and Savior died upon the cross, there was a dry, hard wind—and I saw it was wondrous cold.

The blessed body dried for a long time and alone with the piercing of the nails and the weight of the body. For I understood that with the size of the nails and their grievous hardness bearing into the tenderness of the sweet hands and the sweet feet, the wounds opened wider and the body sagged for all its weight during the long time it was hanging here; and what with this piercing and the wringing of the head

with lightness of the crown, all became baked
dry with blood. . . . To see all these many pains
of Christ filled me with pain. I knew well enough
that he suffered it only the once, but he wanted
to show me his sufferings and to fill me with
mind of it as I had begged him at the outset.[28]

SALVE SANCTA FACIES

All hail! O holiest human face, wherein
we find the shining trace from Heaven above;
Buyer-again of souls grown dark with sin,
brightest blood-price, paid for us, best love-token,
image taken for the wounded winding shroud to
      show:
taken and returned on fabric white as blazing
      snow.
All hail! Worship of all Worlds that are, or are to be:
Mirror of all saints and mortal image true,
immortal angels covet for to see
the blessed fellowship we hold of you.
Cleanse us of every vice's speck or spark;
All hail! Our joy through life grown hard and dark,
sliding, fragile, O so quickly made to pass:
Hail, blessed face glimpsed darkly through our glass!

Lead us to Christ's true country, nearby and clear,
where his saving visage does appear:
a lightning help, defending us from darkest harms,
counselor sweet no enemy has ever vexed.
At rest within our truest Lover's arms,

be for us cause of all joy in this world and the next,
as all do say, "So be it; Amen! Amen!"
now and for ever, then, and once again, we do say,
    "Amen!"

Dolores Warwick Frese[29]

The Face of Jesus on the Holy Shroud

One of the most remarkable relics of the passion, death, and resurrection of Jesus is the Holy Shroud of Turin. This venerable relic reveals for us the innumerable marks of the terrible flogging Jesus underwent, the awful evidence left by the crown of thorns, the dreadful nail holes in his hands and feet, the streams of blood that ran down his face, arms, and upper body, and, most memorably, his majestic and disfigured face.

A Devotion to the Holy Shroud of Turin

LEADER: Christ's head † was as white as wool,
        alleluia!
ALL: ~HIS FACE LIKE THE SUN SHINING WITH
        FULL FORCE, ALLELUIA!
LEADER: Christ is victor, Christ is ruler,
ALL: ~CHRIST IS LORD OF ALL.

A HYMN OF THE PASSION

The head that once was crowned with thorns
Is crowned with glory now;
A royal diadem adorns
The mighty victor's brow.

The highest place that heaven affords
Is his by sov'reign right,
The King of kings, the Lord of lords,
All heaven's eternal light.

The joy of all who dwell above
The joy of all below
To whom he manifests his love,
And grants his name to know;

To them the cross, with all its shame,
With all its grace, is given;
Their name, and everlasting name,
Their joy, the joy of heaven.

They suffer with their Lord below;
They reign with him above;
Their profit and their joy to know
The mystery of his love.

The cross he bore is life and health,
Though shame and death to him;
His people's hope, his people's wealth,
Their everlasting theme!

Thomas Kelly (1769–1854)[30]

PSALM 27:1, 4–10, 13–14   MY LIGHT AND MY SALVATION

The leader of prayer begins the antiphon to the asterisk, and the group completes it.

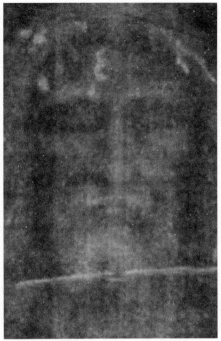

Shroud of Turin (detail)

ANTIPHON "Come," my heart says, *
  "SEEK THE LORD'S FACE."

The Lord is my light and my salvation;
  whom shall I fear?
  The Lord is the strength of my life;
  of whom shall I be afraid?

One thing I asked of the Lord,
  that will I seek after;
that I may dwell in the house of the Lord
  all the days of my life,
to behold the beauty of the Lord
  and to inquire in the Lord's temple.

The Lord will hide me in a shelter,
  in the day of my trouble;
will conceal me under the cover of a tent
  and will set me high upon a rock.

Now my head is lifted up
  above my enemies round about me;
and I will offer sacrifices in the Lord's tent
  with shouts of joy;
I will sing and make melody to the Lord.

Hear, O Lord when I cry aloud,
  be gracious to me and answer me!
"Come," my heart says, "seek the Lord's face."
  Your face, Lord, do I seek.

Do not hide your face from me.
  Do not turn your servant away in anger,
  you who have been my help.
Do not cast me off, do not forsake me,
  O God of my salvation!

I believe that I shall see the goodness of the Lord
  in the land of the living!
Wait for the Lord;
  be strong, and let your heart take courage.
    Wait for the Lord!

All repeat the antiphon.

ANTIPHON "COME," MY HEART SAYS,
  "SEEK THE LORD'S FACE."

PSALM PRAYER
LEADER: Let us pray (*pause for quiet prayer*):

Innocent Jesus,
lying witnesses accused you falsely,
faithless priests sentenced you to death,
and craven Pilate sent you to your death:
By the help of the Holy Shroud,
help us to contemplate your bitter sufferings
and appraise your love and trust in us,
now and for ever.
ALL: ~AMEN.

A Reading from the Gospel according to Saint John 19:38–42

Reader: Joseph of Arimathea, who was a disciple of Jesus, though a secret one because of fear of the Jews, asked Pilate to let him take away the body of Jesus. Pilate gave permission; he came and removed the body [from the cross]. Nicodemus, who had at first come to Jesus by night, also came, bringing a mixture of myrrh and aloes, weighing about a hundred pounds. They took the body of Jesus and wrapped it with the spices in linen cloths, according to the burial custom of the Jews. Now there was a garden in the place where he was crucified, and in the garden there was a new tomb in which no one had ever been laid. And so, because it was the Jewish Day of Preparation, and the tomb was nearby, they laid Jesus there.

Pause for quiet prayer

Responsory

Leader: Having bought a linen cloth, Joseph took him down.

All: ~Having bought a linen cloth, Joseph took him down.

Wrapped him in the linen cloth and laid it in the tomb.

~Having bought a linen cloth, Joseph took him down.

Glory to the Father, and to the Son, and to the
Holy Spirit:
~HAVING BOUGHT A LINEN CLOTH, JOSEPH TOOK
HIM DOWN.

THE CANTICLE OF THE SUFFERING SERVANT

ISAIAH **49:16; 50:6–7; 52:13–15; 53:2–12**

The leader of prayer begins the antiphon to the
asterisk, and the group completes it.

ANTIPHON See, I have inscribed you * ON THE PALMS
OF MY HANDS.

I gave my back to those who struck me,
  and my cheeks to those who pulled out my beard;
I did not hide my face from insult and spitting.

The Lord GOD helps me;
  therefore I have not been disgraced;
therefore I have set my face like flint,
  and I know that I shall not be put to shame;
he who vindicates me is near.

See my servant shall prosper;
  he shall be exalted and lifted up,
  and shall be very high.
Just as there were many who were
  astonished at him
  —so marred was his appearance,
    beyond human semblance,
  and his form beyond that of mortals—
so he shall startle many nations;

He had no form or majesty that
    we should look at him,
nothing in his appearance that
    we should desire him.

He was despised and rejected by others;
    a man of suffering and acquainted with
            infirmity;
And as one from whom others hide their faces;
    he was despised, and we held him of no account.

Surely he has borne our infirmities
    and carried our diseases;
yet we accounted him stricken,
    struck down by God, and afflicted.

But he was wounded for our transgressions,
    crushed for our iniquities;
upon him was the punishment that made us
            whole,
    and by his bruises we are healed.

To the One seated on the throne and to the Lamb
    be blessing and honor and glory and might
    for ever and ever. Amen.

All repeat the antiphon.

ANTIPHON SEE, I HAVE INSCRIBED YOU ON THE PALMS
OF MY HANDS.

Shorter Devotions

A Litany of the Victorious Cross

LEADER: We adore you, Lord Jesus Christ,
as you mounted your victorious Cross.

ALL: ~MAY THIS CROSS DELIVER US FROM THE
AVENGING ANGEL.

We adore you wounded body as it was taken down
from the cross by Joseph and Nicodemus.
~MAY YOUR WOUNDS BE OUR HEALING.

We adore you as you were laid in your mother's lap.
~SHE ALONE PERSISTED IN FAITH AND HOPE ON
HOLY SATURDAY.

We adore you as your disciples observed
the burial customs of the Jews.
~MAY WE BE COMPASSIONATE AS JOSEPH AND
NICODEMUS.

We adore you as they wrapped you in the linen
shroud and put you in the new tomb in
which no one had ever been laid.
~MAY WE VENERATE YOUR HOLY SHROUD AND
VALUE YOUR SUFFERINGS.

We adore you as you descend among the dead
to enlighten and deliver them.
~MAY YOUR DEATH BE OUR LIFE.

We adore your glorious rising from the dead
  on the third day.
~Free us from all fear of death everlasting.

We adore you ascending to the right hand of your
      Father.
~Raise us to eternal glory with all your
      saints.

We adore you presenting your precious wounds
  to the Father through all eternity.
~Rescue us from all our sins.

We adore you coming in glory to judge
  the living and the dead.
~At your gracious coming be not our judge
      but our Savior.

Pause for our special intentions.

By the prayers of Our Lady of Sorrows,
  the Beloved Disciple, and of all the women
  facing the cross,
~Deliver us from all sin and sorrow.

The Lord's Prayer
Leader: Lord, have mercy.
All: ~Christ, have mercy. Lord, have mercy.

Our Father in heaven (all in unison):

Closing Prayer
Leader: Lord Jesus Christ, wrapped in a linen
      shroud and laid in noble Joseph's new

tomb in the garden where you were
crucified: By the precious blood accenting
the shroud, and by the many wounds
scarring your body, may we be led through
your death and burial and be brought to
your glorious resurrection that rescues us
from the death that lasts for ever.

ALL: ~AMEN.

LEADER: Lord Jesus, show us your face,
ALL: ~AND WE SHALL BE SAVED.

BLESSING
LEADER: May the glorious passion of our Lord Jesus
Christ ✝ bring us to the joys of Paradise.
ALL: ~AMEN.

Our Lord's Passion
In your hour of holy sadness
Could I share with you, what gladness
Should your cross to me be showing.
Gladness past all thought of knowing,
  Bowed beneath your cross to die!

Blessed Jesus, thanks I render
That in bitter death, so tender,
You now hear your supplicant calling;
Save me, Lord, and keep from falling
  From you, when my hour is nigh.

St. Bernard of Clairvaux (1090–1153)[31]

A Fourteenth-Century Meditation on the Passion

O good Jesus,
nailed to the cross, crowned with thorns,
given gall to drink, pierced with a lance,
and for my sake dislocated in all thy limbs
   upon the gibbet of the cross:
How greatly thou hast loved me,
since whereas thou art thyself most good,
for me thou hast desired to be reckoned
   among the wicked;
being thyself most beautiful,
   for me thou hast desired to be accounted
   as a leper and the last of men;
being thyself strong and powerful,
   for me thou didst allow thyself
   to be executed like a thief;
being thyself wise, for me thou didst desire
   to be the butt of mocking words and gestures
   from those who stood around the cross,
and so all that was within or without thee
   caused thee suffering for my sake.
Alas! that head, an object of awe to angelic powers,
   is pierced with sharpest thorns;
the face on which the angels desire to gaze
     (1 Peter 1:12)
   is spat upon with vile mouths;
the hands which fashioned heaven and earth

are pierced with sharp nails;
the heart that knows all the secret things of God
    is laid bare when the side is opened;
the belly from which there flows living waters
        (John 7:38)
    is contracted with hunger and pain;
the back which supports heaven and earth
    is beaten and torn with stripes;
the reins which extinguish all impurity
    are stripped and scourged;
the legs which have wrought pleasure for men
    are held fast by the points of nails;
the feet whose footstool is the universe
    are nailed to the cross;
the soul, which from the first moment of its creation
    had full fruition of the Godhead,
    is sorrowful unto death.

Dom John Whiterig (✝ 1371)[32]

The Book

"Study then, O man, to know Christ: get to
know your Savior. His body, hanging on the cross,
is a book, open for your perusal. The words of this
book are Christ's actions, as well as his sufferings
and passion, for everything that he did serves
for our instruction. His wounds are the letters or
characters, the five chief wounds being the five
vowels and the others the consonants of your

book. Learn how to read the lamentations and alas! too, the reproaches, outrages, insults, and humiliations which are written therein."

Dom John Whiterig († 1371)[33]

The Angel of the Agony

Jesu! by that shuddering dread which fell on Thee;
Jesu! by that cold dismay which sicken'd Thee;
Jesu! by that pang of heart which thrill'd in Thee;
Jesu! by that mount of sins which crippled Thee;
Jesu! by that sense of guilt which stifled Thee;
Jesu! by that innocence that girded Thee;
Jesu! by that sanctity that reign'd in Thee;
Jesu! by that Godhead which was one with Thee;
Jesu! spare those souls which are so dear to Thee;
Who in prison, calm and patient, wait for Thee;
Hasten, Lord, their hour, and bid them come to
        Thee,
To that glorious Home, where they shall ever gaze
        on Thee.

Blessed John Henry Cardinal Newman (1801–1890)[34]

The Sorrowing Virgin

Today, O Christ, that pure and spotless virgin gazes upon you, as you hang on the wood of the cross, O Word of God, and in the agony of her cruelly wounded soul she weeps bitterly, wringing her hands as she cries out to you in her anguish:

How can it be, O my Son, divine light of the world, how can it be that you fade from my sight, O Lamb of God? Where is that handsome beauty of yours, that gentle countenance? My heart cannot bear the sight of you on this cross! O Lord, beyond our comprehension, glory to you![35]

A Litany to Our Lady of Sorrows

Lord, have mercy	~LORD, HAVE MERCY
Christ, have mercy	~CHRIST, HAVE MERCY
Lord, have mercy	~LORD, HAVE MERCY
God our Father in heaven	~HAVE MERCY ON US
God the Son, Redeemer of the world	~HAVE MERCY ON US
God the Holy Spirit	~HAVE MERCY ON US
Holy Trinity, one God	~HAVE MERCY ON US
Holy Mary, Mother of God,	~PRAY FOR US.
Mother of the Crucified,	~PRAY FOR US.
Mother standing under the Cross,	~PRAY FOR US.
Afflicted Mother,	~PRAY FOR US.
Mother transfixed with a sword of sorrow,	~PRAY FOR US.
Mother bereaved of your Son,	~PRAY FOR US.
Mother constant on Holy Saturday,	~PRAY FOR US.
Strength of believers,	~PRAY FOR US.
Joy of the sorrowful,	~PRAY FOR US.
Consolation of the afflicted,	~PRAY FOR US.
Refuge of the abandoned,	~PRAY FOR US.
Shield of the oppressed,	~PRAY FOR US.
Solace of the wretched of the earth,	~PRAY FOR US.
Medicine of the sick,	~PRAY FOR US.
Help of the faint-hearted,	~PRAY FOR US.
Companion of the down-hearted,	~PRAY FOR US.

Comfort of the despairing,	~PRAY FOR US.
Courage of the dying,	~PRAY FOR US.
Treasure of the faithful,	~PRAY FOR US.
Joy of all the saints on earth,	~PRAY FOR US.
Queen of all the saints and angels,	~PRAY FOR US.

Pray for us, most Sorrowful Virgin,
~THAT WE MAY BECOME WORTHY OF THE
    PROMISES OF CHRIST.

Let us pray:

Lord Jesus Christ,
in whose bitter Passion,
according to the prophecy of old Simeon,
a sword of sorrow pierced the heart of your dear
    Mother:
Please grant that we who recall her seven sorrows
may obtain the fruit of your death on the Cross.
Your reign is a reign for all ages.
~AMEN.[36]

4
Resurrection and Ascension

The completion of the Paschal Mystery is found in the glorious Resurrection of our Lord and in his wonderful Ascension that made possible the coming of the Holy Spirit.

> The Second Vatican Council (1962–1965) agreed with the Council of Trent that the Mass was rightly described as a sacrifice united with the sacrifice of Christ on the cross, but Vatican II went further by explicitly including the Resurrection in it, as the fullness of the "Paschal Mystery."[37]

As a result of this fresh emphasis both preaching and popular devotions began to shift from a stress on the Passion to an insistence on the inclusion of all the facets of the full Paschal Mystery.

An Easter Sermon of St. Gregory the Theologian

Yesterday I was crucified with him; today I am glorified with him. Yesterday I died with him;

today I am made alive with him. Yesterday I was buried with him; today I am raised up with him. Let us offer to him who suffered and rose again for us . . . ourselves, the possession most precious to God, and most proper. Let us become like Christ, since he became like us. Let us become divine for his sake, since for us he became man. He assumed the worst that he might give us the better. He became poor that by his poverty we became rich. He accepted the form of a servant that we might win back our freedom.

He came down that we might be lifted up. He was tempted that through him we might conquer. He was dishonored that he might glorify us. He died that he might save us. He ascended that he might draw us, who were thrown down through the fall of sin, to himself. Let us give all, offer all, to him who gave himself as ransom and reconciliation for us. We needed an incarnate God, a God put to death, that we might live. We were put to death together with him that we might be cleansed. We rose again with him because we were put to death with him. We were glorified with him because we rose again with him. A few drops of blood recreate the whole universe.

Saint Gregory Nazianzus (ca. 329–390)[38]

A Homily of Saint Cyril of Jerusalem (ca. 313–386)

What a strange and astonishing situation! We did not really die, we were not really buried, we did not really hang from a cross and rise again. Our imitation was symbolic, but our salvation a reality. Christ truly hung from a cross, was truly buried, and truly rose again. All this he did gratuitously for us, so that we might share his sufferings by imitating them, and gain salvation in actuality. What transcendent kindness! Christ endured nails in his innocent hands and feet, and suffered pain; and by letting me participate in the pain without anguish or sweat, he freely bestows salvation on me. God, who has brought you from death to life, can grant you the power to walk in newness of life (Romans 6:4).

Pascha: Jesus Is Raised from the Dead

> "We are Easter people and alleluia is our song."
> **Saint Augustine of Hippo Regius (354–430)**

The resurrection of Jesus is the dominant mystery of the Christian faith and the very center of the Christian year. Let us rejoice and be glad, alleluia!

> Jesus alone
> is master of Egypt, Greece, and Rome,
> Judea, and Persia. With every breath
> let the quick, the sick, and the dead praise Him
> who has conquered death.
>
> **Aurelius Prudentius Clemens (348–ca. 410)**[39]

This following devotion is for Easter Day itself, for the whole of Easter Week, and for every Sunday in Eastertide.

A Visit to the Empty Tomb on Easter Morning

Quem quaeritis
("Whom Do You Seek?")

One of the most affecting Easter devotions began in monasteries, cathedrals, and parishes of the Middle Ages either at the ending of the Mattins of Easter Sunday or at the beginning of Mass on Easter morning.

It was a ritual play of words and gestures that portrayed the meeting between the angel of the Resurrection and the three myrrh-bearing women.

THE ANGEL: As the three women approach the tomb carrying spices to anoint the body of Jesus, he asks:

~"Whom are you looking for? Do not be alarmed; you are looking for Jesus of Nazareth, who was crucified. He has been raised; he is not here."

THE THREE WOMEN REPLY: ~"Alleluia! He has risen. Alleluia!"

THE ANGEL: ~"Look, there is the place they laid Him.

THE WOMEN: ~"Yes, indeed, He has truly risen.

THE ANGEL: ~"Go, tell his disciples and Peter that He is going ahead of you to Galilee; there you will see him just as he told you."

So they left the tomb quickly with fear and great joy and ran to tell His disciples.

Suddenly Jesus met the three women and said, "Greetings!" And they came to him, took hold of his feet, and worshipped him. Then Jesus said to them, "Do not be afraid; go and tell my brothers to go to Galilee; there they will see me."

Now the eleven disciples went to Galilee, to the mountain to which Jesus had directed them. And Jesus came to them and said to them:

"All authority in heaven and on earth has been given to me. Go therefore and make disciples of all nations, baptizing them in the name of the Father and of the Son and of the Holy Spirit, and teaching them to obey everything that I have commanded you."

ALL: ~Alleluia, Alleluia, Alleluia!

On the Lord's Day, the visit above may be used to replace the opening verses and Psalm 117; see in brackets below.

O Lord, **✝** open my lips,
~And my mouth shall declare your praise.
Christ is risen, alleluia!
~He is risen indeed, alleluia!

The leader begins the first antiphon to the
asterisk, and the group says the alleluia. Then
the leader recites the psalm verses, and the group
repeats the antiphon each time.

PSALM 117   A CALL TO PRAISE AND PRAYER

ANTIPHON Christ the Lord has risen, * ALLELUIA!
Praise the Lord, all you nations!
Give glory, all you peoples!
The Lord's love for us is strong;
the Lord is faithful for ever.

ANTIPHON CHRIST THE LORD HAS RISEN, ALLELUIA!
Glory to the Father, and to the Son,
and to the Holy Spirit:
as it was in the beginning, is now,
and will be for ever. Amen.

ANTIPHON CHRIST THE LORD HAS RISEN, ALLELUIA!

A HYMN FOR EASTER
Who is this who comes in triumph,
Clothed in royal garments dyed with blood,
Walking in the greatness of his glory,
Bearing in his hand the holy rood?

This is Christ the risen Lord, the Strong One,
He who trod the winepress all alone;
Out of death he comes with life unending,
Seeking those he purchased for his own,

Great and wonderful is our Redeemer,
Christ the living One, the just, the true.
Praise him with the Father and the Spirit,
Ever with us, making all things new.[40]

1. Reading   New Birth   1 Peter 1:1–5
Blessed be the God and Father of our Lord Jesus
Christ, who in his great mercy gave us a new
birth to a living hope through the resurrection of
Jesus Christ from the dead, to an inheritance that
is imperishable, undefiled, and unfading, kept
in heaven for you who by the power of God are
safeguarded through faith, to a salvation that is
ready to be revealed in the final time.

Pause for quiet prayer

Responsory
Very early on the first day of the week,
the women went to the tomb, alleluia!
~Very early on the first day of the week,
the women went to the tomb, alleluia!

Who will roll back the stone for us from the
            entrance to the tomb?

Do not be alarmed; you are looking for Jesus of
    Nazareth, who was crucified.
~VERY EARLY ON THE FIRST DAY OF THE WEEK,
THE WOMEN WENT TO THE TOMB, ALLELUIA!

He has been raised; he is not here.
Look, there is the place they laid him.
~VERY EARLY ON THE FIRST DAY OF THE WEEK,
THE WOMEN WENT TO THE TOMB, ALLELUIA!

Glory to the Father, and to the Son,
and to the Holy Spirit:
~VERY EARLY ON THE FIRST DAY OF THE WEEK,
THE WOMEN WENT TO THE TOMB, ALLELUIA!

2. A READING OF
POPE LEO THE GREAT   **OUR HUMAN FLESH**

"We are celebrating Easter in vain unless we are
firmly convinced that what we see hanging on the
cross is our own human flesh, and that in Jesus, as
the first fruits, the whole human race has already
been raised to life. It was our human flesh that lay
in the tomb, our human flesh that rose again on
the third day, and our human flesh that ascended
above the heavens to the Father's right hand. Jesus
had only one aim in all that he did and suffered:
our salvation."[41]

See the Responsory on page 105.

3. A Reading of Jacques Maritain on the Passion and the Resurrection

"The Passion of Good Friday is no doubt ordered to the glory of Easter, pledge of the glory of all the elect, and of the transfiguration of the world. . . . If, in the couple Passion-Resurrection, Easter appears as a supreme accomplishment, it is because, inseparable from Good Friday, Easter, far from effacing the latter, presupposes it and contains it, by causing the scandal of God nailed to the wood to emerge into the exaltation of God risen and of the creature saved; the joy of Easter, insofar as joy of the victory over death, is a dazzling crown of pure silver on the bloody gold of Good Friday."[42]

Pause for quiet prayer

Responsory

Blessed be the God and Father of our Lord Jesus
    Christ,
~Blessed be the God and Father of our Lord
    Jesus Christ.

Who in his great mercy gave us a new birth to a
    living hope.
~Blessed be the God and Father of our Lord
    Jesus Christ.

Glory to the Father, and to the Son,
    and to the Holy Spirit:

~Blessed be the God and Father of our Lord
Jesus Christ.

THE GREATER DOXOLOGY

Glory to God in the highest
and on earth peace to people of good will.

We praise you,
we bless you,
we adore you,
we glorify you,
we give you thanks for your great glory,
Lord God, heavenly King,
O God, almighty Father.

Lord Jesus Christ, Only Begotten Son,
Lord God, Lamb of God, Son of the Father,
you take away the sins of the world,
   have mercy on us;
you take away the sins of the world,
   receive our prayer;
you are seated at the right hand of the Father,
   have mercy on us.

For you alone are the Holy One,
you alone are the Lord,
you alone are the Most High,
Jesus Christ,
with the Holy Spirit,
in the glory of God the Father. Amen.[43]

AN EASTER LITANY

Risen Christ, only Son of our Father in heaven,
~HEAR US AND HELP US, WE HUMBLY PRAY.
Risen Christ, who died for our sins,
~HEAR US AND HELP US, WE HUMBLY PRAY.
Risen Christ, who rose for our justification,
~HEAR US AND HELP US, WE HUMBLY PRAY.
Risen Christ, put to death in the flesh,
    raised to life in the Spirit,
~HEAR US AND HELP US, WE HUMBLY PRAY.

Risen Christ, who descended among the dead
    to set them free,
~HEAR US AND HELP US, WE HUMBLY PRAY.

Risen Christ, seated at the Father's right hand
    in glory,
~HEAR US AND HELP US, WE HUMBLY PRAY.

Risen Christ, who washes the whole world clean
    in the waters of Holy Baptism,
~HEAR US AND HELP US, WE HUMBLY PRAY.

Risen Christ, you are the hope and glory of all
    who believe in you,
~HEAR US AND HELP US, WE HUMBLY PRAY.

We pray for our special intentions.

Risen Christ, by the prayers of the great Mother of
        God, Mary most holy, and of all the saints
        in glory,
~HEAR US AND HELP US, WE HUMBLY PRAY.

THE LORD'S PRAYER

Lord, have mercy.

~CHRIST, HAVE MERCY. LORD, HAVE MERCY.

Our Father in heaven, (all in unison):

CLOSING PRAYER

Lord Jesus Christ,
by your glorious resurrection,
you trampled down death
and brought life to those in the grave.
May your blessed passion
be the joy of the whole world
and your rising from the tomb
ever be our song of praise,
O Savior of the world,
living and reigning with the Father,
in the unity of the Holy Spirit,
one God, for ever and ever.

~AMEN.

Christ has risen, alleluia!

~HE HAS RISEN, INDEED, ALLELUIA!

The Five Hours of the Resurrection: A Little Office of the Risen Christ

The Lord's Day: He Has Risen as He Promised!

One of the earliest accomplishments of the apostolic age was the choice of the first day of the week to celebrate the Lord's Supper on the Lord's Day. Long before there was an Easter Sunday proper or a Pentecost Sunday to conclude the great fifty days of Eastertide, Sunday had become the weekly celebration of the glorious Resurrection of our Lord, God, and Savior, Jesus Christ.

This devotion has five full 'Hours': Mattins/Vigils, Morning Praise/ Lauds, Noon Hour, Vespers/Evensong, and Night Prayer. Some people will be able to pray all the Hours each day. Many others will be able to pray a few Hours or perhaps only one each day. In any case they all provide a taste of the Resurrection.

Mattins/Vigils

LEADER: O Lord, ✝ open my lips,

ALL: ~AND MY MOUTH SHALL DECLARE YOUR PRAISE.

LEADER: This is the day which the Lord has made;

ALL: ~LET US REJOICE AND BE GLAD.

PSALM 117   A CALL TO PRAYER NAB

ANTIPHON Enter God's courts * WITH PRAISE!

Praise the Lord, all you nations!
  Give glory, all you peoples!
The Lord's love for us is strong;
  The Lord is faithful for ever.

~ENTER GOD'S COURTS WITH PRAISE!

Glory to the Father, and to the Son,
  and to the Holy Spirit:
as it was in the beginning, is now,

and will be for ever. Amen.

~Enter God's courts with praise!

Ode 1 of the Great Canon of St. John of Damascus

O Day of resurrection!
Let us beam with festive joy!
This, indeed, is the Lord's own Passover,
for from death to life, from earth to heaven
Christ has led us
as we shout the victory hymn!

~Christ has risen from the dead!

Let our hearts be spotless
as we gaze upon our spotless Christ:
Behold his rising, a brilliant flash of light divine!
Let us listen, clearly hear him greeting us,
as we shout the victory hymn!

~Christ has risen from the dead!

Let all heaven burst with joy!
Let all earth resound with gladness!
Let all creation dance in celebration!
For Christ has risen, Christ, our lasting joy!

~Christ has risen from the dead![44]

Psalm 66:1–9, 16–20   His Awesome Deeds

Antiphon Christ is risen from the dead *
conquering death by his death,

AND GIVING LIFE TO THOSE IN THE GRAVE,
ALLELUIA!

Make a joyful noise to God, all the earth;
  sing the glory of God's name;
  give glory to God's praise!

Say to God, "How awesome are your deeds!
  Because of your great power, your enemies
    cringe before you.
All earth worships you:
  they sing praises to you,
  sing praises to your name."

Come and see what God has done:
  God is awesome in deeds among mortals.
God turned the sea into dry land.
  they passed through the river on foot.

There we rejoiced in God
  who rules by might forever,
whose eyes keep watch on the nations—
  let the rebellious not exalt themselves.

Bless our God, O peoples,
  let the sound of God's praise be heard,
who has kept us among the living,
  and has not let our foot slip.

Come and hear, all you who worship God,
  and I will tell what God has done for me.
I cried aloud to God,
  who was highly praised with my tongue.

If I had cherished iniquity in my heart,
  the Lord would not have listened.
But truly God has listened,
  and has given heed to the voice of my prayer.
Blessed be God,
  who has not rejected my prayer
  or removed steadfast love from me.

ANTIPHON CHRIST IS RISEN FROM THE DEAD,
  CONQUERING DEATH BY HIS DEATH,
  AND GIVING LIFE TO THOSE IN THE GRAVE,
  ALLELUIA!

PSALM PRAYER
LEADER: Let us pray (*pause for silent prayer*):

Christ our God, Lord of life and death,
raised from the tomb by your Father:
Be the conqueror for our sake
and for the sake of all our friends
who live in the mercy of God
and the glorious resurrection
that you promised and achieved.
Your reign is a reign for all ages.
ALL: ~AMEN.

1. THE SPICE-BEARING WOMEN   MARK 16:1–7
When the sabbath was over, Mary Magdalene, and
Mary the mother of James, and Salome bought
spices so that they might go and anoint him. And

very early on the first day of the week, when the sun had risen, they went to the tomb. They had been saying to one another, "Who will roll away the stone for us from the entrance to the tomb?" When they looked up, they saw that the stone, which was very large, had already been rolled back. As they entered the tomb, they saw a young man, dressed in a white robe, sitting on the right side; and they were alarmed. But he said to them, "Do not be alarmed; you are looking for Jesus of Nazareth, who was crucified. He has been raised; he is not here. Look, there is the place they laid him. But go, tell his disciples and Peter that he is going ahead of you to Galilee; there you will see him, just as he told you. So they went out and fled from the tomb, for terror and amazement had seized them; and they said nothing to anyone, for they were afraid.

(Other Gospel accounts for succeeding Sundays: Mark 16:9–20; Matthew 28:1–10/16–20; Luke 24:1–12/13–35/36–53; John 20:1–10/11–18/19–31; 21:1–14.)

Pause for silent prayer

RESPONSORY
LEADER: Christ is risen from the dead, alleluia!
ALL: ~CHRIST IS RISEN FROM THE DEAD, ALLELUIA!

He is risen indeed, alleluia!

~CHRIST IS RISEN FROM THE DEAD, ALLELUIA!

Glory to the Father, and to the Son
  and to the Holy Spirit:

~CHRIST IS RISEN FROM THE DEAD, ALLELUIA!

2. READING   JESUS AND PETER   JOHN 21:4–14

Just after daybreak, Jesus stood on the beach; but
the disciples did not know that it was Jesus. Jesus
said to them, "Children, you have no fish, have
you? They answered him, "No." He said to them,
"Cast to the right side of the boat, and you will
find some." So they cast it, and now they were not
able to haul it in because there were so many fish.
That disciple whom Jesus loved said to Peter, "It is
the Lord!" When they had gone ashore, they saw
a charcoal fire there, with fish on it, and bread.
Jesus said to them, "Bring some of the fish that
you have just caught." Jesus said to them, "Come
and have breakfast." Now none of the disciples
dared to ask him, "Who are you?" because they
knew it was the Lord. Jesus came and took the
bread and gave it to them, and did the same
with the fish. This was the third time that Jesus
appeared to the disciples after he was raised from
the dead.

Pause for silent prayer

RESPONSORY

Christ has risen from the tomb, alleluia!

~CHRIST HAS RISEN FROM THE TOMB, ALLELUIA!

Who for our sake hung on the cross.

~CHRIST HAS RISEN FROM THE TOMB, ALLELUIA!

Glory to the Father, and to the Son,
  and to the Holy Spirit:

~CHRIST HAS RISEN FROM THE TOMB, ALLELUIA!

THE CANTICLE OF THE CHURCH

We praise you, O God,
we acclaim you as Lord;
all creation worships you,
the Father everlasting.

To you all angels, all the powers of heaven,
the cherubim and seraphim, sing in endless praise:

  Holy, holy, holy Lord, God of power and might,
  heaven and earth are full of your glory.

The glorious company of apostles praise you.
The noble fellowship of prophets praise you.
The white-robed army of martyrs praise you.

Throughout the world the holy Church acclaims
        you:
  Father of majesty unbounded,
  your true and only Son, worthy of all praise,
  the Holy Spirit, advocate and guide.

You, Christ, are the king of glory,

the eternal Son of the Father.
When you took our flesh to set us free
you humbly chose the Virgin's womb.

You overcame the sting of death,
and opened the kingdom of heaven to all believers.
You are seated at God's right hand in glory.
We believe that you will come to be our judge.

Come, then Lord, and help your people,
bought with the price of your own blood,
and bring us with your saints
to glory everlasting.

St. Nicetas of Remesiana (ca. 335–414)[45]

CLOSING PRAYER

Heavenly Father, Lord of life and death,
when Christ our paschal lamb was sacrificed,
he overcame death by his own dying
and restored us to life by his own rising.
In virtue of his life-giving Passover,
pour your Holy Spirit into our hearts,
fill us with awe and reverence for you,
and with love and compassion for our neighbor.
We ask this through the same Christ our Lord.

ALL: ~AMEN.

Christ is risen from the dead *
conquering by his death,

~AND GIVING LIFE TO THOSE IN THE GRAVE,
        ALLELUIA!

Blessing

May Christ, the King of Glory,
who overcame the sting of death,
† bless us and keep us.
~Amen.

Morning Praise/Lauds

O God, † come to my assistance.
~O Lord, make haste to help me.
Lead the festal procession with branches, alleluia!
~Up to the horns of the altar, alleluia!

Ode 5 of the Great Canon of St. John of Damascus

Now at daybreak let us celebrate!
Let us gaze on Christ, our sun of holiness!
Instead of spices, let us offer him our song,
as he brings forth life for all!

Hell's captives saw your endless mercy
and fled to you, their light!
And on their lips the happy news:
Christ, our God, has truly risen!
Clap your hands!
Applaud the lasting Passover!

Come, let us all go forth to meet him!
Let us welcome our triumphant Christ!
Today, he bursts the tomb in glory,
God's own Passover, our souls' salvation!

With heaven's powers let us celebrate
this greatest of all festivals,
filled with joy and gladness.[46]

	1 Corinthians 5:7–8;
Christ Our	**Romans 6:9–11;**
Paschal Lamb	**1 Corinthians 15:20–22**

Antiphon Thanks be to God, * who gives us the
victory through our Lord Jesus Christ,
alleluia!

Christ, our paschal lamb, has been sacrificed.
 Therefore let us celebrate the festival,
not with the old yeast, the yeast of malice and evil,
 but with the unleavened bread of sincerity and
 truth. Alleluia!

Christ being raised from the dead, will never die
 again;
 death no longer has dominion over him.
The death he died, he died to sin, once for all;
 but the life he lives, he lives to God.
So also you must consider yourselves dead to sin
 and alive to God in Christ Jesus. Alleluia!

Christ has been raised from the dead,
 the first-fruits of those who have died.
For since death came through a human being,
 the resurrection of the dead has also come
 through a human being;
for as all die in Adam,

so all will be made alive in Christ. Alleluia!

Glory to the Father, and to the Son,
  and to the Holy Spirit:
as it was in the beginning, is now,
  and will be for ever. Amen.

ANTIPHON THANKS BE TO GOD, WHO GIVES US THE
  VICTORY THROUGH OUR LORD JESUS CHRIST,
  ALLELUIA!

PSALM PRAYER

Let us pray (*pause for quiet prayer*):

Lord Jesus Crucified and Risen,
your five precious wounds
in hands, feet, and side
are like rubies in your sacred body:
By these marks made visible,
rescue us from the pains of death,
even when we are laid in dust and the grave.
Your reign, O Lord of the world, is a reign
  for all ages.
~AMEN.

1. READING   CHRIST IS RISEN   ACTS 10:38–41

Jesus went about doing good and healing all who
were oppressed by the devil, for God was with
him. We are witnesses to all that he did both in
Judea and in Jerusalem. They put him to death by
hanging him on a tree; but God raised him on the

third day and allowed him to appear, not to all the people but to us who were chosen by God as witnesses, and who ate and drank with him after he rose from the dead.

Pause for silent prayer

RESPONSORY

Thanks be to God who has given us the victory, alleluia!

~THANKS BE TO GOD WHO HAS GIVEN US THE VICTORY, ALLELUIA!

Through our Lord Jesus Christ, alleluia!

~THANKS BE TO GOD WHO HAS GIVEN US THE VICTORY, ALLELUIA!

Glory to the Father, and to the Son, and to the Holy Spirit:

~THANKS BE TO GOD WHO HAS GIVEN US THE VICTORY, ALLELUIA!

2. A READING FROM THE HOLY GOSPEL OF SAINT JOHN 21:15–17

When they [the disciples on the beach] had finished breakfast, Jesus said to Simon Peter, "Simon son of John, do you love me more than these?" He said to him, "Yes, Lord; you know I love you." Jesus said to him, "Feed my lambs." At a second time he said to him, "Simon son of John, do you love me?" He said to him, "Yes, Lord; you know that I love you." Jesus said to him, "Tend my sheep." He said to him the third time, "Simon son of John, do you love me?" Peter felt hurt because he said to him the third time, "Do you love me?" And he said to him, "Lord, you know everything; you know that I love you." Jesus said to him, "Feed my sheep."

Pause for silent prayer

RESPONSORY

You are the Messiah, the Son of the Living God.

~YOU ARE THE MESSIAH, THE SON
    OF THE LIVING GOD.

You are Peter, and on this rock I will build my
    church.

~YOU ARE THE MESSIAH, THE SON
    OF THE LIVING GOD.

Glory to the Father, and to the Son,
  and to the Holy Spirit:

~YOU ARE THE MESSIAH, THE SON
    OF THE LIVING GOD.

THE GREATER DOXOLOGY

Glory to God in the highest
and on earth peace to people of good will.

We praise you,
we bless you,
we adore you,
we glorify you,

we give you thanks for your great glory,
Lord God, heavenly King,
O God, almighty Father.

Lord Jesus Christ, Only Begotten Son,
Lord God, Lamb of God, Son of the Father,
you take away the sins of the world,
  have mercy on us;
you take away the sins of the world,
  receive our prayer;
you are seated at the right hand of the Father,
  have mercy on us.

For you alone are the Holy One,
you alone are the Lord,
you alone are the Most High,
Jesus Christ,
with the Holy Spirit,
in the glory of God the Father. Amen.[47]

A LITANY OF THANKSGIVING

Thanks be to God for the mighty resurrection
  of his only Son, our Savior:
~THANKS BE TO GOD.

Thanks be to God for the forty days Jesus spent
  with his apostles and disciples:
~THANKS BE TO GOD.

Thanks be to God for the many convincing proofs
  Jesus gave of his risen life:
~THANKS BE TO GOD.

Thanks be to God for his constant speaking
about the kingdom of God:
~THANKS BE TO GOD.

Thanks be to God for the Lord's final commission
to his apostles to baptize all nations:
~THANKS BE TO GOD.

Thanks be to God for Christ's wondrous ascension
into heaven:
~THANKS BE TO GOD.

Thanks be to God for the promised Paraclete
Spirit.
~THANKS BE TO GOD.

Pause for our special intentions.

Thanks be to God for the abiding faith of Holy
Mary and the other women from Galilee:
~THANKS BE TO GOD.

THE LORD'S PRAYER
Let us pray as Jesus taught us:

Our Father in heaven, (all in unison):

CLOSING PRAYER
Abba, dear Father,
you lifted your beloved Son from the grave
and made him a beacon of hope for all mortals.
By overcoming sin and death and hell,
may he take us by the hand

and conduct us into the land of bliss and glory
where we shall enjoy for ever
the company of the whole heavenly host.
May we trust with all our hearts
  in his glorious wounds
by which he ransomed us for everlasting life.
Blessed be the name of Jesus, now and for ever.
~AMEN.

Let us bless the Lord, alleluia, alleluia!
~THANKS BE TO GOD, ALLELUIA, ALLELUIA!

BLESSING
May our radiant and dazzling Christ
✝ lead us from death to life,
from earth to heaven.
~AMEN.

Full Life
Christ banner guides us on Christ's way,
the royal way of him who died!
O wondrous Cross from which began
our life when Life was crucified.

Noonday Hour/Sext
O God, ✝ come to my assistance.
~O LORD, MAKE HASTE TO HELP ME.
I shall not die, but I shall live, alleluia!
~AND RECOUNT THE DEEDS OF THE LORD,
    ALLELUIA!

ODE 8 OF THE GREAT CANON OF ST. JOHN OF DAMASCUS

That hallowed day has come!
Of all holy Sabbaths first and foremost!
The very expectation of God's people:
Festival of festivals, of all solemnities, the greatest,
when all of us bless Christ forever!

That hallowed, chosen day has come!
Let us share this joy divine!
Let us taste the vine's new fruit
and share the lasting reign of Christ
when all of us bless him forever!

Rise up, Zion! Lift your eyes!
See your children here before you!
How they beam with light divine!
From all corners of the earth
your scattered sons and daughters come to you!
See how they hasten to your bosom,
where all of us bless Christ forever![48]

PSALM 118:1, 13–17, 21–24, 28–29   THE EMPTY TOMB

ANTIPHON The stone which the builders rejected *
HAS BECOME THE CORNERSTONE, ALLELUIA!

O give thanks to the Lord, who is good;
whose steadfast love endures forever!

I was pushed hard, so that I was falling,
but the Lord helped me.

The Lord is my strength and my power;
   the Lord has become my salvation.

There are joyous songs of victory
   in the tents of the righteous:
"The right hand of the Lord does valiantly,
   the right hand of the Lord is exalted,
   the right hand of the Lord does valiantly!"

I shall not die, but I shall live,
   and recount the deeds of the Lord.
I thank you that you have answered me
   and have become my salvation.

The stone which the builders rejected
   has become the cornerstone.
This is the Lord's doing;
   it is marvelous in our eyes.
This is the day which the Lord has made;
   let us rejoice and be glad.

You are my God, and I will give thanks to you;
   you are my God, I will extol you.
I give thanks to the Lord, who is good;
   for God's steadfast love endures forever!

ANTIPHON THE STONE WHICH THE BUILDERS
   REJECTED HAS BECOME THE CORNERSTONE,
   ALLELUIA!

PSALM PRAYER
Let us pray (*pause for quiet prayer*):

Abba, dear Father,
by the grace of the risen Christ,
who died that we might live
and who slept that we might keep watch,
may we reign with him in glory,
in the life that knows no end;
through the same Christ our Lord.
~Amen.

MATTHEW
28:8–10

READING   **GO TO GALILEE**

The women left the tomb with fear and great joy,
and ran to tell his disciples. Suddenly Jesus met
them and said, "Greetings!" And they came to
him, took hold of his feet, and worshipped him.
Then Jesus said to them, "Do not be afraid; go
and tell my brothers to go to Galilee; there they
will see me."

Pause for silent prayer

RESPONSORY

Christ is risen from the dead, alleluia!
~CHRIST IS RISEN FROM THE DEAD, ALLELUIA!

And became our blessed Savior.
~CHRIST IS RISEN FROM THE DEAD, ALLELUIA!

Glory to the Father, and to the Son,
    and to the Holy Spirit:
~CHRIST IS RISEN FROM THE DEAD, ALLELUIA!

CLOSING PRAYER

Holy, mighty, and immortal God,
in raising Jesus from the dead
you restored the whole world
to its pristine condition
and freed us from sin and error.
May we rejoice and dance for joy
in the Eastertide of our existence
and live for ever in your embrace.
We ask this through our risen Savior.
~AMEN.

Christ is risen, alleluia, alleluia!
~HE IS RISEN, INDEED, ALLELUIA, ALLELUIA!

AN ANTIPHON OF THE CROSS

Holy Cross, *
YOU ARE MORE EXALTED THAN ALL THE TREES
   OF THE FOREST:
ON YOU HUNG THE LIFE OF THE WORLD;
ON YOU CHRIST PROCEEDED TO HIS TRIUMPH;
ON YOU DEATH OVERCAME DEATH. ALLELUIA!

The Lord reigns from the tree, alleluia!
~TREMBLE BEFORE HIM, ALL THE EARTH,
         ALLELUIA!

Let us pray:

Almighty and everlasting God,
grant that we who believe

that your only-begotten Son, our Savior,
rose from the dead and ascended into heaven,
may ourselves dwell in spirit amid heavenly things;
through the same Christ our Lord.
~Amen.

Evensong/Vespers

Light and peace ✝ in Jesus Christ our Lord.
~Thanks be to God.
I lie down and sleep, alleluia!
~I wake again, for the Lord sustains me,
    alleluia!

Ode 9 of the Great Canon of Saint John of Damascus

My soul tells out the greatness of Christ,
the font and source of life,
for he has risen on the third day
from the darkness of the tomb.

Shine forth in splendor, new Jerusalem!
The Lord's bright glory bursts upon you!
Skip for joy in happy festival, O Zion!
And you, O purest one!
Rejoice with us, O Theotokos!
For Christ, your Son, has risen!

My soul tells out the greatness of him
who freely suffered and died,
who was buried and rose on the third day
from the darkness of the tomb!

Shine forth in splendor, new Jerusalem!
The Lord's bright glory bursts upon you!
Skip for joy in happy festival, O Zion!
And you, O purest one!
Rejoice with us, O Theotokos!
For Christ, your son, has risen!

An angel greeted you, O full of grace:
O purest virgin, rejoice!
And again I say: Rejoice!
For your Son has risen from the grave,
and with himself has raised the dead.
People everywhere, rejoice![49]

PSALM 139:1–12   THE DIVINE PRESENCE

ANTIPHON Christ is risen from the dead *
  CONQUERING BY HIS DEATH, AND GIVING LIFE
  TO THOSE IN THE GRAVE, ALLELUIA!

O Lord, you have searched me and known me!
  You know me when I sit down and when I rise up;
  you discern my thoughts from afar.

You search out my path and my lying down,
  and are acquainted with all my ways.
Even before a word is on my tongue, O Lord,
  you know it completely.

You pursue me behind and before,
  and lay your hand upon me.
Such knowledge is too wonderful for me;
  it is so high, I cannot attain it.

Where shall I go from your spirit?
  Or where shall I flee from your presence?
If I ascend to heaven, you are there!
  If I make my bed in Sheol, you are there!

If I take the wings of the morning
  and dwell in the deepest parts of the sea,
even there your hand shall lead me,
  and your right hand shall hold me.

If I say, "Let only darkness cover me,
  and the light about me be night,"
even darkness is not dark to you,
  the night is bright as day;
  for darkness is as light with you.

ANTIPHON CHRIST IS RISEN FROM THE DEAD
  CONQUERING BY HIS DEATH, AND GIVING LIFE
  TO THOSE IN THE GRAVE, ALLELUIA!

PSALM PRAYER

Let us pray (*pause for quiet prayer*):

All-knowing God and Father,
you have fearfully and wonderfully made
the risen Christ our Savior.
Rule and guide our hearts
to worship his presence
now and for ever.
~AMEN.

Mary Magdalene
1. Reading   and Jesus   John 20:11–18

Mary stood weeping outside the tomb. As she wept, she bent over to look into the tomb; and she saw two angels in white, sitting where the body of Jesus had been lying, one at the head and the other at the feet. They said to her, "Woman why are you weeping?" She said to them, "They have taken away my Lord, and I do not know where they have laid him." When she had said this, she turned around and saw Jesus standing there, but she did not know that it was Jesus. Jesus said to her, "Woman, why are you weeping? Whom are you looking for?" Supposing him to be the gardener, she said to him, "Sir, if you have carried him away, tell me where you have laid him, and I will take him away." Jesus said to her, "Mary!" She turned and said to him in Hebrew, "Rabbouni!" (which means Teacher). Jesus said to her, "Do not hold on to me, because I have not ascended to the Father. But go to my brothers and say to them, "I am ascending to my Father and your Father, to my God and your God." Mary Magdalene went and announced to the disciples, "I have seen the Lord"; and she told them that he had said these things to her.

Pause for silent prayer

RESPONSORY

We adore your Cross, O Lord, and we praise
   and glorify your holy Resurrection.
~WE ADORE YOUR CROSS, O LORD, AND
      WE PRAISE AND GLORIFY YOUR HOLY
      RESURRECTION.

By the wood of the Cross, joy came
   into the whole world.
~WE ADORE YOUR CROSS, O LORD, AND
      WE PRAISE AND GLORIFY YOUR HOLY
      RESURRECTION.

Glory to the Father, and to the Son,
   and to the Holy Spirit.
~WE ADORE YOUR CROSS, O LORD, AND
      WE PRAISE AND GLORIFY YOUR HOLY
      RESURRECTION.

2. READING   SHALOM!   JOHN 20:19–23

When it was evening on that day, the first day
of the week, and the doors of the house where
the disciples had met were locked for fear of the
Jews, Jesus came and stood among them and said,
"Peace be with you." After he said this, he showed
them his hands and his side. Then the disciples
rejoiced when they saw the Lord. Jesus said to
them again, "Peace be with you. As the Father has
sent me, so I send you." When he had said this, he
breathed on them, and said to them, "Receive the

Holy Spirit. If you forgive the sins of any, they are forgiven them; if you retain the sins of any, they are retained."

Pause for silent prayer

RESPONSORY

I was dead, and see that I am alive for ever and
      ever.

~I WAS DEAD, AND SEE THAT I AM ALIVE
      FOR EVER AND EVER.

I have the keys of Death and of Hades.

~I WAS DEAD, AND SEE THAT I AM ALIVE
      FOR EVER AND EVER.

Glory to the Father, and to the Son,
   and to the Spirit:

~I WAS DEAD, AND SEE THAT I AM ALIVE
      FOR EVER AND EVER.

3. READING   **THE APPEARANCES OF CHRIST**   **1 CORINTHIANS 15:1–8**

Now I would remind you, brothers and sisters, of the good news that I proclaimed to you, which you in return received, in which also you stand, through which also you are being saved, if you hold firmly to the message that I proclaimed to you—unless you have come to believe in vain. For I handed on to you as of first importance what I in turn had received that Christ died for our sins in accordance with the scriptures, and that he was buried, and that he was raised on the third day in accordance with the scriptures, and that he appeared to Cephas, then to the twelve. Then he appeared to more than five hundred brothers and sisters at one time, most of whom are still alive, though some have died. Then he appeared to James, then to all the apostles. Last of all, as to one untimely born, he also appeared to me.

Pause for silent prayer

RESPONSORY

Christ was raised from death, alleluia!

~CHRIST WAS RAISED FROM DEATH, ALLELUIA!

By the power of the Father, alleluia!

~CHRIST WAS RAISED FROM DEATH, ALLELUIA!

Glory to the Father, and to the Son,
    and to the Spirit:

~CHRIST WAS RAISED FROM DEATH, ALLELUIA!

THE CANTICLE OF THE VIRGIN MARY   LUKE 1:46–55

ANTIPHON Rejoice, O Mary, rejoice today, alleluia! *
THE CLOUDS OF NIGHT HAVE PASSED AWAY,
        ALLELUIA!
THE OFFSPRING OF YOUR VIRGIN WOMB, ALLELUIA!
HAS RISEN FROM THE VIRGIN TOMB, ALLELUIA!

My soul † proclaims the greatness of the Lord,
my spirit rejoices in God my Savior,

for you, Lord, have looked with favor
     on your lowly servant.

From this day all generations will call me blessed:
   you, the Almighty, have done great things for me
   and holy is your name.
   You have mercy on those who fear you,
   from generation to generation.

You have shown strength with your arm
and scattered the proud in their conceit,
casting down the mighty from their thrones
and lifting up the lowly.
You have filled the hungry with good things
and sent the rich away empty.

You have come to the aid of your servant Israel,
to remember the promise of mercy,
the promise made to our forebears,
to Abraham and his children for ever.

Glory to the Holy and Undivided Trinity:
now and always and for ever and ever. Amen.

ANTIPHON REJOICE, O MARY, REJOICE TODAY,
     ALLELUIA!
THE CLOUDS OF NIGHT HAVE PASSED AWAY,
          ALLELUIA!
THE OFFSPRING OF YOUR VIRGIN WOMB, ALLELUIA!
HAS RISEN FROM THE VIRGIN TOMB, ALLELUIA![50]

A LITANY OF THE RESURRECTION

Lord Jesus, who rose again on the third day:
~HEAR US, RISEN LORD.

Lord Jesus, Savior of the world and Ruler
of the new creation:
~HEAR US, RISEN LORD.

Lord Jesus, who established the new
and eternal covenant in your blood:
~HEAR US, RISEN LORD.

Lord Jesus, who set us free from the law
of sin and death:
~HEAR US, RISEN LORD.

Lord Jesus, pleading for us at God's right hand:
~HEAR US, RISEN LORD.

Lord Jesus, the hope of those who die in you:
~HEAR US, RISEN LORD.

Pause for our special intentions.

Lord Jesus, by the prayers of the great Mother of
God, Mary most holy, and of the whole
company of heaven:
~HEAR US, RISEN LORD.

THE LORD'S PRAYER

Lord, have mercy.
~CHRIST, HAVE MERCY. LORD, HAVE MERCY.

Our Father in heaven, (all in unison):

Closing Prayer

Lord Christ, victorious Redeemer,
a new song is sung throughout the world
because of your triumph over death and hell.
Extend your gentle rule over all nations
and prepare us for your awesome coming
to judge the world in might and glory.
You live and reign, now and for ever.
~Amen.

Let us bless the Lord, alleluia, alleluia!
~Thanks be to God, alleluia, alleluia!

May Christ who reigns from the tree of the cross,
✝ bless us and keep us.
~Amen.

Night Prayer/Compline

Our help ✝ is in the name of the Lord,
~The maker of heaven and earth.
I lie down and sleep, alleluia!
~I wake again, for the Lord sustains me,
    alleluia!

Ode 9 of the Great Canon of Saint John of Damascus

When you died, O Lion of Judah,
with your mighty, regal voice
you raised those who had died
from the beginning.

How divine, how mellow!
The voice of purest love,
your promise to remain with us, O Christ,
till the very end of time.
Firmly do we hold to this, your promise,
as the wellspring of our faith and joy!

You are the greatest Passover, O Christ,
  the holiest,
O wisdom, word, and power of God!
Show us your radiant presence, fuller, ever holier,
when you come again in glory, O Lord,
on that day of never-setting sun.

Let all creation rejoice and be glad this day,
for Christ has risen and destroyed the power of
          hell!
Rejoice, O Virgin Mary, most pure and blessed
          Lady!
Rejoice, for your Son has risen on the third day
from the darkness of the grave![51]

Psalm 22:22–30   Christ Reigns and Rules

Antiphon Those who seek the Lord *
  shall praise the Lord!
I will tell of your name to my kindred;
  in the midst of the congregation I will praise you;
All who fear the Lord, shout praise!
  All you offspring of Jacob, glorify God!
  Stand in awe, all you offspring of Israel!

For God did not despise or abhor,
  the affliction of the afflicted,
nor hide from me,
  but heard when I cried out.

From you comes my praise
  in the great congregation;
my vows I will pay before those
  who worship the Lord.

The poor shall eat and be satisfied;
  those who seek the Lord shall praise the Lord!
  May your hearts live forever!

All the ends of the earth shall remember
  and turn to the Lord;
and all the families of the nations
  shall worship before the Lord.
For dominion belongs to the Lord,
  who rules over the nations.

All who are prosperous in the land
  shall eat and bow down to the Lord.
All who go down to the dust
  shall bow before the Lord,
  for they cannot keep themselves alive.

Posterity shall serve the Lord;
  each generation shall tell of the Lord,
and proclaim deliverance to a people yet unborn:
  surely the Lord has done it.

ANTIPHON THOSE WHO SEEK THE LORD
SHALL PRAISE THE LORD!

PSALM PRAYER

Let us pray (*pause for quiet prayer*):

Lord God Almighty,
you manifested your power and glory
when Jesus, your beloved Son,
dealt death a deathblow
and brought life to those in the grave.
May all the earth remember and turn to you,
paying their vows with profound thanksgiving.
We ask this through the same Christ our Lord.
~AMEN.

	THE	**MATTHEW**
READING	**GREAT COMMISSION**	**28:16–20**

The eleven disciples went to Galilee, to the
mountain to which Jesus had directed them.
When they saw him, they worshipped him; but
some doubted. And Jesus came and said to them,
"All authority in heaven and on earth has been
given to me. Go therefore and make disciples of
all nations, baptizing them in the name of the
Father and of the Son and of the Holy Spirit, and
teaching them to obey everything that I have
commanded you. And remember, I am with you
always, to the end of the age."

Pause for silent prayer

Responsory

Holy, holy, holy Lord, God of power and might,
~HOLY, HOLY, HOLY LORD, GOD OF POWER AND
   MIGHT,

Heaven and earth are full of your glory.
~HOLY, HOLY, HOLY LORD, GOD OF POWER AND
   MIGHT,

Glory to the Father, and to the Son,
   and to the Holy Spirit:
~HOLY, HOLY, HOLY LORD, GOD OF POWER AND
   MIGHT.

A Homily of Saint Augustine of Hippo Regius: Ascension

"After He arose from the dead He ascended into
heaven and sits at the right hand of the Father.
Perhaps you still did not believe this. Listen to the
Apostle who says, 'He who descended is the same
one who ascended far above all the heavens, so
that he might fill all things' (Ephesians 4:10). Take
heed lest you experience the wrath of Him whose
resurrection you would refuse to accept. 'Those who
do not believe are condemned' (John 3:18). For he
who is now seated at the right hand of the Father as
our advocate, shall come to judge the living and the
dead. Therefore, let us believe, for 'whether we live or
whether we die, we are the Lord's' (Romans 14:8)."[52]

Pause for silent prayer

RESPONSORY

A light to reveal you to the nations

~A LIGHT TO REVEAL YOU TO THE NATIONS.

And the glory of your people Israel.

~A LIGHT TO REVEAL YOU TO THE NATIONS.

Glory to the Father, and to the Son,
    and to the Holy Spirit:

~A LIGHT TO REVEAL YOU TO THE NATIONS.

THE CANTICLE OF
SIMEON THE PROPHET   LUKE 2:29–32 ELLC

ANTIPHON CHRIST HAS RISEN FROM THE DEAD *
    CONQUERING DEATH BY HIS DEATH,
    AND BRINGING LIFE TO THOSE IN THE GRAVE.

Now, Lord, **†** let your servant go in peace:
your word has been fulfilled.

My own eyes have seen your salvation
which you have prepared in the sight
    of every people:

a light to reveal you to the nations
and the glory of your people Israel.

Glory to the Father, and to the Son,
    and to the Holy Spirit:
as it was in the beginning, is now,
    and will be for ever. Amen.

Antiphon Christ has risen from the dead,
   conquering death by his death,
   and bringing life to those in the grave.

Closing Prayer
Saving God,
when your Son cried out to you
from the cross of pain and humiliation,
you lifted him out of the sleep of death
and exalted him to your right hand.
By the grace of his glorious resurrection
   and wondrous ascension,
uphold your people, shield us from our enemies,
and bring us home with him
to the resurrection of the body and the life
      everlasting;
we ask this through Christ Jesus, our risen Lord.
~Amen.

Let us bless the Lord, alleluia, alleluia!
~Thanks be to God, alleluia, alleluia!

Blessing
By the precious and life-giving cross,
may our risen Lord † save us and keep us.
~Amen.

A Marian Anthem for All Eastertide
Rejoice, O Queen of Heaven, alleluia! *
For the Son you bore, alleluia!

Has arisen as He promised, alleluia!
Pray for us to God the Father, alleluia!

Rejoice and be glad, alleluia!
~For the Lord has really risen, alleluia!

Let us pray:

Holy, mighty, and living God,
you have given joy to the world
by the resurrection of your Son,
   our Lord Jesus Christ.
Through the prayers of his Mother,
   the Virgin Mary,
and of the whole company of heaven,
bring us to the joys of everlasting life;
We ask this through the same Christ our Lord.
~Amen.[53]

A Devotion to the Risen Christ

The Paschal Mystery culminates in the resurrection and ascension of Jesus Christ our Lord. By sharing his death by our dedication to his life and death and by sharing his new life by embracing his life-giving sacraments, we personally belong to the people of God and walk with them on our lifelong pilgrimage to our heavenly home. Alleluia!

1. Risen Christ, Lord of life and death,
you emerged from noble Joseph's tomb
by the will and power of your dear Father,

and created the new people of God.
~Glory to you, O Lord, glory to you!

2. Risen Christ, Lord of life and death,
as you rose in the midst of an earthquake,
the guards shook and became like dead men,
and you stepped into the splendor of your rising.
~Glory to you, O Lord, glory to you!

3. Risen Christ, Lord of life and death,
on Easter morning Mary Magdalene
saw that the stone had been removed,
and ran to tell Peter and the beloved disciple.
~Glory to you, O Lord, glory to you!

4. Risen Christ, Lord of life and death,
Peter and John ran to the tomb together,
viewed the empty linen wrappings,
and saw and believed.
~Glory to you, O Lord, glory to you!

5. Risen Christ, Lord of life and death,
as Mary stood weeping outside the tomb,
you called her by name, and said to her,
"I am ascending to my Father and your Father,
  to my God and your God."
~Glory to you, O Lord, glory to you!

You are looking for Jesus of Nazareth, alleluia!
~He has risen, he is not here, alleluia!

Holy, mighty, and living God,
joy came into the world
when your raised your dear Son
   from among the dead.
By the prayers of Mary his Mother,
Mary Magdalene, the beloved disciple,
and of all the other women from Galilee,
raise us up with Jesus, the victor over death,
and bring us to the happiness of everlasting life;
through the same Christ our Lord.
~AMEN.

6. Risen Christ, Lord of life and death,
the Mary who had stood near the cross
became the apostle of the apostles,
by witnessing your living presence
to the men whom you had called.
~GLORY TO YOU, O LORD, GLORY TO YOU!

7. Risen Christ, Lord of life and death,
on Easter evening you came
and stood among your apostles
and said, "Peace be with you!"
and showed them your hands and your side.
~GLORY TO YOU, O LORD, GLORY TO YOU!

8. Risen Christ, Lord of life and death,
on Easter evening you opened the Scriptures
and made yourself known in the breaking of bread

to two of your disciples on the road to Emmaus.
~Glory to you, O Lord, glory to you!

9. Risen Christ, Lord of life and death,
you appeared to the apostles
  by the lake of Galilee,
and confirmed their faith
by eating and drinking with them.
~Glory to you, O Lord, glory to you!

10. Risen Christ, Lord of life and of death,
you said to Thomas the Apostle,
"Put your finger here and see my hands;
reach out your hand and put it into my side.
Do not doubt but believe."
~Glory to you, O Lord, glory to you!

Christ has been raised from the dead, alleluia!
~And will never die again, alleluia!

Prayer
Risen Lord Jesus,
your life and death have passed over
into the sacraments of the Church,
the life-giving memorials of your presence.
In the Holy Eucharist may we touch by faith
your risen body and its five glorious wounds,
O Savior of the world,
living and reigning with the Father,
in the unity of the Holy Spirit,

one God, for ever and ever.
~Amen.

11. Risen Christ, Lord of life and death,
you appeared to Peter, then to the twelve;
then to five hundred brothers and sisters at one time;
then you appeared to James, then
    to all the apostles.
~Glory to you, O Lord, glory to you!

12. Risen Christ, Lord of life and death,
you came and said to your disciples,
"All authority in heaven and on earth
  has been given to me.
Go and make disciples of all nations."
~Glory to you, O Lord, glory to you!

13. Risen Christ, Lord of life and death,
you said to them, "Baptize them
and teach them to obey everything
that I have commanded you."
~Glory to you, O Lord, glory to you!

14. Risen Christ, Lord of life and death,
you ordered your disciples not to leave Jerusalem
but wait there for the promise of the Father,
and then become your witnesses to the end
    of the earth.
~Glory to you, O Lord, glory to you!

15. Risen Christ, Lord of life and death,
lifting up your hands, you blessed your disciples,

withdrew from them, and were carried up
      into heaven.
They worshipped you, and returned to Jerusalem
  with great joy.
~GLORY TO YOU, O LORD, GLORY TO YOU!

Thanks be to God who gives us the victory,
      alleluia!
~THROUGH OUR LORD JESUS CHRIST, ALLELUIA!

PRAYER
God our Rescuer,
you heard your dear Son
when he cried out to you
in pain and humiliation on the cross,
and then raised him from the sleep of death.
By the power of his glorious resurrection
and his wonderful ascension,
uphold your chosen people,
shield us from our enemies,
and bring us home in safety at the last.
We ask this through the same Christ our Lord.
~AMEN.

BLESSING
May the grace of our Lord Jesus Christ,
and the love of God, and the communion
  of the Holy Spirit,
✝ be with us all, now and for ever.
~AMEN.

5
The Ascension of Christ

As a conclusion to the great transit of mercy, the Lord Jesus returns to his Father in triumph. He is the King of Glory, the Life of the new creation, the Giver of the Spirit, the Sovereign of the cosmos, our only Mediator. He makes us "a chosen race, a royal priesthood, a holy nation, God's own people" (1 Peter 2:9). The famous and early theologian Saint Irenaeus of Lyons (ca. 130–ca. 200), and the two main creeds of the Catholic Church make the same affirmations of the Paschal Mystery:

The Church though disseminated throughout the world, even to the ends of the earth, received from the apostles and their disciples the faith in one God the Father Almighty, the Creator of heaven and earth, and the seas and all things that are in them; and in the one Jesus Christ, the Son of God who was enfleshed for our salvation; and in the Holy Spirit, who through the prophets preached the Economies, the coming, the birth from a Virgin, the passion, the resurrection from the dead, and the bodily ascension into heaven of the beloved Son, Christ Jesus our Lord, and his coming from heaven in the glory of the Father to recapitulate all things, and to raise up all flesh of the whole human race. . . . The Church, as we have said above, though disseminated throughout the whole world, carefully guards this preaching and this faith which she has received, as if she dwelt in one house. She likewise believes these things as if she had but one soul and one and the same heart; she preaches, teaches, and hands them down harmoniously, as if she possessed one mouth.

St. Irenaeus of Lyons[54]

Christ comes † to fill the whole universe, alleluia!

~WITH HIS GLORIOUS PRESENCE, ALLELUIA!

You are seated at God's right hand in glory.

~WE BELIEVE THAT YOU WILL COME TO BE OUR JUDGE.

HYMN

Hail the day that sees him rise,
To his throne above the skies;
Christ, a while to mortals given,
Reascends his native heaven.

There for him high triumph waits;
Lift your heads, eternal gates;
He has conquered death and sin;

Take the King of glory in.

Highest heaven its Lord receives,
Yet he loves the earth he leaves:
Though returning to his throne,
Still he calls us all his own.

See he lifts his hands above;
See, he shows the prints of love;
Hark, his gracious lips bestow
Blessings on his Church below.[55]

PSALM 47   THE ASCENSION

ANTIPHON God has gone up * WITH A SHOUT,
ALLELUIA!

Clap your hands, all peoples!
  Shout to God with loud songs of joy!
For the Lord, the Most High, is to be feared,
  a great Ruler over all the earth,
who subdued peoples under us,
  and nations under our feet,
who chose our heritage for us,
  the pride of Jacob whom God loves.

God has gone up with a shout,
  the Lord with the sound of a trumpet.
Sing praises to God, sing praises!
  Sing praises to our Ruler, sing praises!
For God is Ruler of all the earth;
  sing praises with a psalm!

God reigns over the nations;
  God sits on a holy throne.

The princes of the people gather
  as the people of the God of Abraham.
For the shields of the earth belong to God,
  who is highly exalted!

ANTIPHON GOD HAS GONE UP WITH A SHOUT,
ALLELUIA!

PSALM PRAYER
Let us pray (*pause for quiet prayer*):

Lord Most High,
Ruler of all the earth,
exalt your divine Son
among all earth's peoples
and bring them into subjection
to the perfect law of love.
Blessed be Jesus, true God and true Man.
~AMEN.

1. READING	TRANSFORMATION OF CREATION	REVELATION 21:1–5

I saw a new heaven and a new earth; for the first
heaven and the first earth had passed away, and
the sea was no more. And I saw the holy city, the
new Jerusalem, coming down out of heaven from
God, prepared as a bride adorned for her husband.
And I heard a loud voice from the throne saying,

"See the home of God is among mortals.
He will dwell with them as their God;
they will be his peoples,
and God himself will be with them;
he will wipe away every tear from their eyes.
Death will be no more;
mourning and crying and pain will be no
    more,
for the first things have passed away."
And the One who was seated on the throne said,
    "See, I am making all things new."

Pause for silent prayer

RESPONSORY

Holy, holy, holy is the Lord God almighty,
  who was, and who is, and who is to come.
~HOLY, HOLY, HOLY IS THE LORD GOD ALMIGHTY,
  WHO WAS, AND WHO IS, AND WHO IS TO COME.

Christ is coming amid the clouds,
  and every eye will see him.
~HOLY, HOLY, HOLY IS THE LORD GOD ALMIGHTY,
  WHO WAS, AND WHO IS, AND WHO IS TO COME.

Glory to the Father, and to the Son,
  and to the Holy Spirit.
~HOLY, HOLY, HOLY IS THE LORD GOD ALMIGHTY,
  WHO WAS, AND WHO IS, AND WHO IS TO COME.

2. A Reading from a Gelasian Sacramentary of the Eighth Century

"The time has come for that that we have longed for; what greater or better work than can be found than to proclaim the might of our Risen Lord? Bursting open the doors of the grave, He has displayed to us the glorious banner of His Resurrection. Through Him the children of light are born to life eternal; the courts of the kingdom of heaven are opened to believers; and by the law of blessed intercourse, earthly and heavenly are interchanged. For by the Cross of Christ we have all been redeemed from death, and by His Resurrection the life of us all has risen again. While He has assumed our mortal nature, we acknowledge him as the God of majesty; and in the majesty of the Godhead we confess Him God and Man: Who by dying destroyed our death and by rising again restored our life,—even Jesus Christ our Lord."[56]

Pause for silent prayer

Responsory

Let all creation dance in celebration, alleluia!
~Let all creation dance in celebration, alleluia!

For Christ has risen, Christ our lasting joy.

~Let all creation dance in celebration,
Alleluia!

Glory to the Father, and to the Son,
and to the Holy Spirit.
~Let all creation dance in celebration,
Alleluia!

Pause for silent prayer

3. A Reading from
the Vatican Council II　　　The Heavenly Liturgy

In the earthly liturgy we take part in a foretaste
of that heavenly liturgy which is celebrated in the
holy city of Jerusalem toward which we journey as
pilgrims, where Christ is sitting at the right hand
of God, minister of the sanctuary and of the true
tabernacle (see Revelation 21:2; Colossians 3:1;
Hebrews 8:2). With all the hosts of heaven we sing a
hymn of glory to the Lord; venerating the memory
of the saints, we hope to share their company; we
eagerly await the Savior, Our Lord Jesus Christ, until
he our life shall appear and we will appear with him
in glory (Philippians 3:20; Colossians 3:4).[57]

Pause for silent prayer

Responsory

When the Son of man comes in his glory,
and all the angels with him,
~When the Son of man comes in his glory,
and all the angels with him,

Then he will sit on the throne of his glory.

~When the Son of man comes in his glory,
and all the angels with him,

Glory to the Father, and to the Son,
and to the Holy Spirit:

~When the Son of man comes in his glory,
and all the angels with him,

A Pauline Canticle   1 Timothy 3:16 TEV

Antiphon Praise the Lord, all you nations! *
Praise God, all you peoples!

Jesus Christ appeared in human form,
was shown to be right by the Spirit,
and was seen by angels.

Antiphon Praise the Lord, all you nations!
Praise God, all you peoples!

He was preached among the nations,
was believed in the world,
and was taken up to heaven.

Antiphon Praise the Lord, all you nations!
Praise God, all you peoples!

He is the blessed and only Ruler,
the King of Kings and the Lord of Lords,
he alone is immortal.

Antiphon Praise the Lord, all you nations!
Praise God, all you peoples!

Glory to the Father, and to the Son,
and to the Holy Spirit:
As it was in the beginning, is now,
and will be for ever. Amen.

ANTIPHON PRAISE THE LORD, ALL YOU NATIONS!
PRAISE GOD, ALL YOU PEOPLES!

A LITANY OF THE ASCENSION

Lord Jesus, risen and ascended One:
~BE OUR LIFE AND OUR JOY.

Lord Jesus, culmination of all God's plan:
~BE OUR LIFE AND OUR JOY.

Lord Jesus, the promise made to our ancestors
in the faith:
~BE OUR LIFE AND OUR JOY.

Lord Jesus, fulfillment of the Law and the
Prophets:
~BE OUR LIFE AND OUR JOY.

Lord Jesus, mighty Savior of the whole world:
~BE OUR LIFE AND OUR JOY.

Lord Jesus, giver of the Holy and Life-giving
Spirit:
~BE OUR LIFE AND OUR JOY.

Lord Jesus, Lord of glory and Ruler of the
universe:
~BE OUR LIFE AND OUR JOY.

Pause for our special intentions.

Lord Jesus, by the prayers of the great Mother
of God,
   Mary most holy, and of all the saints in glory:
~Be our life and our joy.

The Lord's Prayer

Lord, have mercy.
~Christ, have mercy. Lord, have mercy.

Our Father in heaven, (*all in unison*):

Closing Prayer

Father in heaven,
our minds were prepared
for the coming of your kingdom
when you took Christ beyond our sight
so that we might seek him in glory.
May we follow where he has led
and find our hope in his ascension,
for he is Lord for evermore.
~Amen.

Let us bless the Lord, alleluia, alleluia!
~Thanks be to God, alleluia, alleluia!

Doxology

To the risen and ascended Christ
be glory both now and to the day of eternity!
~Amen.

An Invocation

Come, Holy Spirit, come!
Come as holy fire and burn in us.
Come as holy wind and cleanse us,
come as holy light and lead us,
come as holy truth and teach us,
come as holy forgiveness and free us,
come as holy love and enfold us,
come as holy power and enable us,
come as holy life and dwell in us.
Convict us, convert us, consecrate us,
until we are wholly yours for your using,
through Jesus Christ our Lord.
~AMEN.[58]

Notes

1. This is the motto of the Carthusian Order.
2. Hans Urs von Balthasar (1905–1988), *The Threefold Garland* (San Francisco: Ignatius Press, 1982), 101.
3. St. Gertrude of Helfta (1256–ca. 1302), *The Herald of Divine Love* (Book III), 42; trans. Margaret Winkworth (New York: Paulist Press, 1993), 210–211.
4. Blessed Julian of Norwich (1342–ca. 1428), *Revelation of Love* (long text), First Revelation, Chapter 6; trans. John Skinner (New York: Image Books/Doubleday, 1997), 122.
5. *The Constitution on the Sacred Liturgy,* Vatican II, chapter 5, "The Liturgical Year"; Austin Flannery, OP, ed. (Northport, NY: Costello Publishing Co., 1996), #109, #151.
6. Peter Ackroyd, *The Life of Thomas More* (New York: Doubleday, 1989), 254.
7. The Monastic Agreement of the Monks and Nuns of the English Nation, Dom Thomas Symons of Downside Abbey, ed. (London: Thomas Nelson and Sons Ltd, 1953), 43–44, translated by William G. Storey.
8. "*The Holy Cross,*" Richard Crashaw (ca. 1613–1649)
9. John Wilkinson, *Egeria's Travels*, third edition. (Warminster, England: Aris and Phillips Ltd., 1999), 155.
10. After St. Ignatius of Antioch († ca. 107), Letter to the Church at Smyrna 1; translated by Cyril C. Richardson, *Early Christian Fathers.* (New York: Macmillan, 1970), 112–113.

11. After Melito, bishop of Sardis (last third of the 2nd century), *On Pascha and other Fragments,* trans. Alistair Stewart-Sykes (Crestwood, NY: St. Vladimir's Seminary Press, 2001), 76, altered.

12. St. Thomas Aquinas, OP (1225–1274), "De passione Christi," *Summa Theologiae* III, 46, 5, (London: Dominican Fathers, 1911), altered by William G. Storey.

13. Blessed Henry Suso, OP (1295–1366), *Little Book of Eternal Wisdom*, chapter 2, trans. Frank Tobin (New York: Paulist Press, 1989), 213–214.

14. Blessed John Henry Newman (1801–1890) "Mental Sufferings of Our Lord in His Passion," from Charles Frederick Harrold, *A Newman Treasury* (New York: Longmans, Green and Co., 1943), 197.

15. St. Augustine of Hippo Regius, On Psalm 55, verse 1, translated by William G. Storey.

16. James Montgomery (1771–1854)

17. Attributed to Thomas à Kempis (ca. 1380–1471), trans. John Mason Neale (1851).

18. Richard Rolle of Hampole (ca. 1300–1349), *Meditations on the Passion,* 36.

19. John Rippon (1751–1836), *A Selection of Hymns* (Chilicothe, OH: J. Hellings, et al., 1815), #477; altered by William G. Storey.

20. Julian of Norwich (ca. 1342–1423), *Showings,* chapter 4, trans. John Skinner (New York: Image Books, Doubleday, 1997), 7–8.

21. Blessed Magaret Ebner, OP (1291–1351), *The Revelations*, translated and edited by Leonard P. Hindsley (New York: Paulist Press, 1993), 95.

22. James Quinn, SJ, *Praise for All Seasons* (Pittsburgh: Selah, 1994), 11.

23. Stanbrook Abbey Hymnal © 1974 and 1995, Callow End, Worcester WR2 4TD.

24. Composed in the eleventh century and used ever since for the Marian antiphon after Compline. *A Book of Prayers* (Washington, DC: ICEL, 1982) 24.

25. Edward Caswall (1814–1878).

26. Attributed to Thomas à Kempis (ca. 1380–1471), translated by John Mason Neale, 1851.

27. James Quinn, SJ, *Praise for All Seasons* (Pittsburgh: Selah, 1994), 18.

28. Blessed Julian of Norwich, *Revelation of Love* (long text), 16 and 17; translated by John Skinner (New York: Image Books, Doubleday, 1997), 35 and 36.

29. *Salve Sancta Facies*, translated by Dolores Warwick Frese, professor of English, the University of Notre Dame. By her permission.

30. "A Hymn of the Passion," Thomas Kelly (1769–1854).

31. "Our Lord's Passion," St. Bernard of Clairvaux (1090–1153).

32. Dom John Whiterig † 1371), solitary of Inner Farne Island and a monk of Durham, "A Meditation Addressed to Christ Crucified," Dom Hugh Farmer, OSB, ed., *The Monk of Farne* (Baltimore, MD: Helicon Press, 1961), chapter 13, pp. 43–44.

33. Dom John Whiterig † 1371), solitary of Inner Farne Island and a monk of Durham, "A Meditation Addressed to Christ Crucified," Dom Hugh Farmer, OSB, ed., *The Monk of Farne* (Baltimore, MD: Helicon Press, 1961), chapter 53, p. 76.

34. "The Angel of the Agony," Blessed John Henry Cardinal Newman (1801–1890), from *The Dream of Gerontius*, 1865. Beatified by Pope Benedict XVI, September 19, 2010.

35. "The Sorrowing Virgin, At Vespers of Holy Saturday," translated by The Monks of New Skete, *Passion and Resurrection* (Cambridge, NY: New Skete, 1995), 187.

36. This litany is derivative of the litany composed by Pope Pius VII (1742–1823) during his imprisonment in France by the Emperor Napoleon.

37. John W. O'Malley, *What Happened at Vatican II* (Cambridge, MA: Harvard University Press, 2010), 295.

38. Saint Gregory Nazianzus (ca. 329–390), *The Life: The Orthodox Doctrine of Salvation,* translated by Clark Carlton (Salisbury, MA: Regina Orthodox Press, 2000), 53–54.

39. Aurelius Prudentius Clemens (348–ca. 410), *Cathemerinon,* "Hymn for Epiphany," translated by David R. Slavit (Baltimore, MD: Johns Hopkins University Press, 1996), 61.

40. "A Hymn for Easter," Based on Isaiah 63:1–7. Stanbrook Abbey Hymnal © 1974 and 1995, Wass, York, YO61 4AY.

41. Pope Leo the Great (✝ 461), Sermons on the Passion, translated by Anne Field, OSB, *The Binding of the Strong Man* (Ann Arbor, MI: Word of Life, 1976), 86.

42. Jacques Maritain, *On the Grace and Humanity of Jesus* (London: Burns & Oates Ltd., 1959), 15.

43. The Greater Doxology, *The Roman Missal.*

44. Ode 1 of the Great Canon of St. John of Damascus (ca. 675–749), translated by the Monks of New Skete, *Passion and Resurrection* (Cambridge, NY: New Skete, 1995), Ode 1, 227.

45. St. Nicetas of Remesiana (ca. 335–414), Te Deum laudamus.

46. Ode 5 of the Great Canon of St. John of Damascus (ca. 675–749), translated by the Monks of New Skete, *Passion and Resurrection* (Cambridge, NY: New Skete, 1995), Ode 5, 230.

47. The Greater Doxology, *The Roman Missal.*

48. Ode 8 of the Great Canon of St. John of Damascus (ca. 675–749), translated by the Monks of New Skete, *Passion and Resurrection* (Cambridge, NY: New Skete, 1995), Ode 8, 234.

49. Ode 9 of the Great Canon of St. John of Damascus (ca. 675–749), translated by the Monks of New Skete, *Passion and Resurrection* (Cambridge, NY: New Skete, 1995), Ode 9, 235–236.

50. Anonymous, twelfth century

51. Ode 9 of the Great Canon of St. John of Damascus (ca. 675–749), translated by the Monks of New Skete, *Passion and Resurrection* (Cambridge, NY: New Skete, 1995), 236–238.

52. Saint Augustine of Hippo Regius (354–430), Sermon 10, "On the Creed to the Candidates for Baptism"; translated by Philip T. Weller, *Selected Easter Sermons of Saint Augustine* (St. Louis, MO: B Herder Book Co., 1959), 221.

53. A twelfth-century antiphon used for the close of Night Prayer during the fifty days of Eastertide; translated by William G. Storey.

54. Saint Irenaeus of Lyons (ca. 130–ca. 200), *The Refutation of Heresies,* Chapter 10, translated by Dominic J. Unger, OFM., Vol. 1, Book 1 (New York: Newman Press, 1992), 48–49.

55. Hymn, Charles Wesley (1707–1788).

56. William Bright, *Ancient Collects and Other Prayers,* 2nd edition, enlarged (Oxford and London: J. H. and Jas. Parker, 1862), 54.

57. *The Constitution on the Sacred Liturgy* 1, 8; ed. Austin Flannery, OP, Vatican Council II (Northport, NY: Costello Publ. Co., 1996), 121.

58. Adapted by Charles Francis Whiston from an ancient prayer in Elizabeth Goudge, *A Diary of Prayer* (New York: Coward-McCann, 1966), 93.

Acknowledgments

Unless otherwise noted, all the Scripture quotations are taken from the New Revised Standard Version Bible: Catholic Edition, copyright © 1989, 1993 National Council of the Churches of Christ in the United States of America. Used by permission. All rights reserved.

Unless otherwise noted, all psalms are taken from *Psalms for Prayer and Worship: A Complete Liturgical Psalter* by John, Holbert et. al. (Nashville, TN: Abingdon Press, 1992).

Two excerpts taken from the *New American Bible with Revised Psalms* © 1991, 1986, 1970 Confraternity of Christian Doctrine, Washington, D.C. and are used by permission of the copyright owner. All rights reserved. No part of the *New American Bible* may be reproduced in any form without permission in writing from the copyright owner.

Two excerpts from *The Good News Bible: Today's English Version* (New York: The American Bible Society, 1992), TEV.

English translations of The Gospel Canticle of Simeon from *Praying Together* © 1988 English Language Liturgical Consultation (ELLC). Used by permission. See: www.englishtexts.org.

English translation of *Salve Regina* from *A Book of Prayers* © 1982, International Commission on English in the Liturgy Corporation (ICEL); two excerpts from the English translation of *The Roman Missal* © 2010 ICEL. All rights reserved.

Three excerpts by Blessed Julian of Norwich (1342–ca. 1428)—two from *Revelation of Love*, one from *Showings*, trans. by John Skinner, translation copyright © 1996 by John Skinner. Used by permission of Image Books/ Doubleday religion, an imprint of the Crown Publishing Group, a division of Random House, Inc. Any third party use of this material, outside of this publication, is prohibited. Interested parties must apply directly to Random House, Inc. for permission.

Three prayers attached to the seven penitential psalms from *The Monastic Agreement of the Monks and Nuns of the English Nation*, Dom Thomas Symons of Downside Abbey, ed. (London: Thomas Nelson and Sons Ltd, 1953). Translated by William G. Storey.

Letter after St. Ignatius of Antioch, trans. by Cyril C. Richardson from *Early Christian Fathers*, Cyril C. Richardson, ed. (New York: Macmillan, 1970).

Prayer after Melito, bishop of Sardis from *On Pascha and other Fragments*, trans. by Alistair Stewart-Sykes (Crestwood, NY: St. Vladimir's Seminary Press, 2001), altered.

Two hymns by James Quinn from *Praise for All Seasons* (Pittsburgh: Selah, 1994).

Salve Sancta Facies, trans. by Dolores Warwick Frese, professor of English, the University of Notre Dame. Used by her permission.

Two meditations by Dom John Whiterig from *The Monk of Farne*, Dom Hugh Farmer, OSB, ed. (Baltimore, MD: Helicon Press, 1961).

"Hymn for Epiphany" by Aurelius Prudentius Clemens (348–ca. 410) from *Cathermerinon*, trans. by David R. Slavit (Baltimore, MD: Johns Hopkins University Press, 1996).

Two hymns from the *Stanbrook Abbey Hymnal* © 1995, 1974, Wass, York. Used with Permission.

The "Sorrowing Virgin, At Vespers of Holy Saturday" and five excerpts from the odes of the Great Canon of St. John of Damascus (ca. 675–749) from *Passion and Resurrection*, trans. by the Monks of New Skete (Cambridge, NY: New Skete, 1995).

Every effort has been made to locate the copyright holders for the works used in this publication and to acknowledge the use of such works. Any mistakes or omissions will be corrected in the next printing of this book.

Prayers or other excerpts without attribution may be considered composed or translated by the author.

About the Author

William G. Storey is professor emeritus of Liturgy and Church History at the University of Notre Dame. He has compiled, translated, and edited many books of prayer, including *A Book of Marian Prayers, A Prayer Book of Catholic Devotions,* and *Novenas.* He currently resides in South Bend, Indiana.